ADALI'S MAGIC

MOLLY'S MAGICAL ADVENTURES: BOOK THREE

V.K. MAY

Copyright © 2021 by V.K. May
All rights reserved.
No part of this book may be reproduced in any form or by any electronic or mechanical means, including information storage and retrieval systems, without written permission from the author, except for the use of brief quotations in a book review. To contact the author, visit: vkmay.com

Published by Opal Tree Press (2021)

Books in this series include:
The Magic Volcano: Book One
Jungle Magic: Book Two
Adali's Magic: Book Three
Magic of the Guardians: Book Four

A NOTE TO READERS

Molly Marsh uses American spelling.

She also uses the metric system which works like this -
   1 meter = 1.1 yards OR 3.3 feet
   1 kilometer = 1,094 yard OR 3,2801 feet
   1 centimeter = 0.4 inch

PROLOGUE

Book Two, <u>Jungle Magic,</u> started with Molly and Michael rushing back into the jungle. Their intention was to sneak into the cave inside the mine and capture a sample of water from the turquoise lake. This, they knew, would help Eddie the journalist prove the lake was contaminated.

But their plan was interrupted by the arrival of a hoard of adults gathering on the path to the mine. Afraid of being seen by them, the kids hid among the foliage for as long as they could. Eventually they gave up and ventured deeper into the jungle. There they encountered several species of plants and animals including a mad daddy cassowary who chased them away from his clutch of eggs. During their terrifying escape, they tripped, fell and rolled down the side of a mountain.

When they awoke in a wide-open valley, sunburnt and dehydrated, they saw a luscious waterfall crashing down a mountain on the far side of the valley. Desperate for shelter and water, they made the trek across the valley. But as they got closer, they realized the waterfall was tumbling straight into a sinkhole. After a careful by magical descent to the bottom, they finally enjoyed some fresh drinking water and cooled down.

While playing in the water, they bumped into something they could not see. Poking it for a few moments, they finally penetrated what turned out to be an invisible wall around a top-secret research facility. They could hardly believe their luck as they gazed around the gigantic dome-shaped greenhouse and its strange botanical experiments. Molly was instantly drawn to a vine growing up the inside of the wall, so she picked one of its bright white flowers.

The next day, she planted the flower in her garden. By that evening, it had grown into a full-sized tree that was invisible during the day and barely visible in the darkness of night. Like the dome in the jungle, the tree was surrounded by a mysterious shield. Molly and Michael broke through the shield and explored the tree for a few moments before being sucked through a hole in its trunk and pulled underground.

Shrunk down to the size of ants, they had no choice but to obey the mycelium network and allow it to take them on a torturous journey through piles of dirt, worms, and darkness. Eventually it lifted them to the surface, inside the dome. There, Molly's curiosity took over and she triggered the alarm. Soon the place was crawling with guards, guns, and dogs. There was no escape. Trapped inside the wall, their only option was to call Adali for help and that's when the magic truly began.

1

THE SLURRY LEACH

The dining table had already been set for lunch, so the only thing Molly had to do was sit down.

'Did you have a nice morning, honey?' her mother asked.

Molly was still trying to understand everything she and Michael had experienced that morning. Breaking through the shield around the magic tree, being shrunk down to the size of ants and dragged underground by the mycelium network had been strange enough. But even stranger was the fact that their absence had only lasted a few minutes when it had felt like a few hours.

'Molly?' her mother said.

'Oh,' said Molly, realizing she had been lost in her thoughts. 'Yes, thanks, Mum. It was great.'

'What did you get up to?' her mother asked, sliding a bowl of salad across the table.

'Michael and I just did some plant research,' Molly lied.

'Yes, I can see you're covered in dirt,' her mother

said. 'Would you please wash your hands and face before eating?'

Molly ran to the bathroom and looked in the mirror. As far as she could see, there was only a small smudge of dirt on her face. But when she leaned over the sink, a pile of dry dirt fell from her hair, completely covering the inside of the sink. It took several minutes to wash it down and then wash herself.

By the time Molly returned to the table, her mother had filled her plate.

'Oh, no,' Molly whispered, staring at the block of lasagna.

'It's completely vegetarian, honey,' her mother said. 'I'll never put meat in front of you again. Don't you worry about that.'

'You're the best mum in the world,' said Molly, sitting down.

From the first bite, she was in heaven. The combination of fresh herbs, tomato, mushroom, and cheese sang a happy song upon her tastebuds.

'Seriously, Mum, you are the *greatest*,' she said.

Her mother winked at her then filled three glasses with cool water.

'Molly, there's something we need to discuss with you,' she said.

'Mm?'

Her father put down his knife and fork and gazed at her.

'Do you remember a few days ago when we were walking toward the mine?' he asked.

'Yes, Dad.'

'Remember when we were walking along that narrow

track?' he asked. 'You were behind me and you asked me why the ground was so damp.'

'Yes,' said Molly. 'Your shoes left a deep imprint in the soil.'

Her father winked at her.

'Well, muppet, it turns out you were really onto something,' he said.

Molly was surprised to hear her father say this because she remembered he had been irritated by her questions during that outing. But he continued.

'You asked me if the slurry might have leached into the surrounding soil and I told you it was not possible because we check the container all the time,' he said.

'That's right,' said Molly. 'I believed you, Dad.'

Her father pressed his lips together so tight that Molly knew he was upset.

'Well, it turns out you were right,' he said. 'The slurry *has* leached into the soil, and it's caused significant damage to the jungle ecosystem.'

Molly jumped up, ready to race into the jungle and see with her own eyes.

'Don't be too quick to react, muppet,' her father said. 'I haven't finished, yet.'

'Okay,' said Molly, sitting down again.

'The guy who discovered the problem wrote an article about it,' her father continued.

'What guy?' Molly asked.

'Eddie someone,' her father replied. 'I can't remember his last name. He's the guy we saw on TV, reporting on the damage caused by the earthquake.'

'Oh, that's Eddie Abaijah,' said Molly.

Her mother's eyebrows lifted.

'That's right, honey,' she said. 'You have a great memory.'

Molly remembered seeing the news report. And she remembered Eddie's face. Suddenly everything started to make sense to her. Eddie must have discovered the slurry leach when he was investigating the cause of the earthquake, she figured. And he would have taken a sample of the slurry, which was why Yosia had told her and Michael not to bother.

'Are you listening to me, muppet?' her father asked.

'Yes, Dad,' said Molly, sitting up straighter.

'Poor Eddie got fired from his job for writing the article,' he said.

'*Fired*?' Molly echoed. 'What does that mean?'

'The news station that employed him forced him to leave,' her father explained.

'Are you saying they were angry with him for telling the truth?' said Molly.

'Yes, muppet, that's exactly what I'm saying,' her father replied. 'When something like that happens, it's usually because someone wants the truth to be kept quiet.'

'Is that because someone did something wrong?' Molly asked.

'Probably,' her father replied.

'That's bad,' said Molly. 'The plants and animals are the most important things on Earth. They were here before us, and we can't live without them.'

Her father nodded.

'I agree with you,' he said. 'And I think there must be a lot of other people who agree with you because the workers in the mine have gone on strike over this.'

'What does *strike* mean?' Molly asked.

'A strike is when people stop working in the hope it will force someone to fix a problem,' her father explained. 'The reason I'm telling you this is because I want you to understand that Mrs. Calthorpe is under a lot of pressure right now.'

Molly remembered the last few times she had seen Mrs. Calthorpe. The woman had been completely stressed out and was very unpleasant to be around.

'Poor Michael,' she whispered. 'No wonder he's had trouble sleeping.'

She suddenly wondered why Michael had rushed home the instant the mycelium network had flung them up to the surface of her garden. Perhaps he had been worrying about his mother and he wanted to make sure she was okay.

'Should we go over there?' Molly asked. 'Just to be sure they're okay, I mean.'

'I think we should,' her father agreed.

'I'm going with you,' said Molly's mother. 'I'd like to offer my support to Philippa during this difficult time.'

2

THE SECRET DOCUMENTS

Molly knocked on the back door of the Calthorpe's house. Almost immediately, it opened. Mrs. Calthorpe stood there looking wild. Her frizzy grey hair was all over the place, as though she had just been electrocuted. The skin under her eyes was dark and her eyes were red.

'Yes?' she said.

'Hi, Philippa,' said Molly's mother. 'We just wanted to make sure you're okay.'

Molly could see Michael standing behind his mother. His hair was sticking out in all directions, his eyes were wide open, the buttons on his shirt were in the wrong buttonholes and he was wearing shoes that did not match.

'Not really,' said Mrs. Calthorpe, stepping out of the house. 'All our workers are on strike.'

'I know,' said Molly's father. 'I was wonder—'

Mrs. Calthorpe put up her hand to stop Molly's father from saying any more.

'Henry wants to see us, so we need to get to the

hospital now,' she said, taking her keys out of her handbag.

'Of course,' said Molly's father, standing back. 'I understand.'

Molly's mother stepped forward and reached toward Mrs. Calthorpe, ready to give the woman a hug, but Mrs. Calthorpe brushed past her and ran down the back steps.

'Come on, Michael!' she shrieked.

Michael followed, without even saying 'hello' or 'goodbye' to Molly.

'Let us know if there's anything we can do to help!' Molly's father called out.

But Mrs. Calthorpe did not reply. She was already in her jeep, putting on her seatbelt. Michael was sitting beside her, trying to flatten his woolly hair with his hands. A moment later, the car reversed down the driveway. And then they were gone.

'Well, that was rude,' said Molly's father.

'It was a bit,' her mother agreed. 'Philippa is obviously under enormous strain.'

'I'm more worried about Michael,' said Molly. 'Putting up with Mrs. Cal—'

'That's enough, muppet,' her father interrupted.

The Marsh family was quick to return to their own garden. As they scuttled past the stilts under their house, Yosia stepped out into the light.

'Sorry to interrupt you, Mr. and Mrs. Marsh,' he said, brushing dust and cobwebs off his shirt.

'No worries, Yosia,' said Molly's father. 'What's up, mate?'

Yosia scratched his head.

'I should have mentioned this earlier, but I'm only

just getting around to it now,' he said. 'Can you see all those cardboard boxes under there?'

Molly and her parents looked at the mass of boxes under the house.

'They belong to Mr. and Mrs. Jeffries,' Yosia explained. 'The American couple who lived in this house before you.'

'Gosh, that's strange,' said Molly's father. 'In a year, they still haven't managed to collect their belongings?'

Yosia shook his head.

'It hasn't been a year,' he said. 'They disappeared about a month before you arrived.'

'A month?' Molly's mother echoed.

'What's in the boxes?' Molly asked.

'That's none of our business,' her mother said.

'I was told the house had been empty for a year,' said Molly's father. 'But if it's only been a few weeks, I'm sure we can keep the boxes here until the Jeffries are ready to collect them.'

Yosia sighed then looked down at the ground.

'They're not coming back, are they?' asked Molly's mother.

'I don't think so,' Yosia replied.

Molly started to feel frustrated. She did not care whose boxes they were or how long they had been there or when they might be collected. She just wanted to know what was in them.

'Can we open them?' she asked.

'No, Molly,' her mother replied. 'It's wrong to invade other peoples' privacy.'

'Hang on,' said Molly's father. 'I'm getting the feeling there might have been something strange about the Jeffries' departure. Was there?'

'I believe so,' Yosia replied. 'One morning, they went to work at the mine. That afternoon, someone from the mine came over and informed me they had left the country. I was told to pack up their belongings and store them here.'

Molly's mother gasped then put her hand over her mouth.

Molly's father scratched his head.

'I think it's important we find out why they left so suddenly,' he said.

'I recall packing several pads of handwritten notes,' said Yosia. 'Perhaps there might—'

'Agreed,' said Molly's father. 'Would you mind unpacking them and giving them to me?'

'Certainly,' said Yosia.

'Thanks, mate,' said Molly's father.

Molly watched her parents return to the house. She felt tempted to follow Yosia under the house and help him poke through the boxes, but then she remembered the huge spider Yosia had chased down there several days earlier. So she sat on the grass and watched the boxes moving. A moment later, the wheelbarrow moved. Then the lawnmower. Eventually, Yosia stepped into a narrow space between the piles of stuff and waved at her.

'Have you found something interesting?' Molly asked.

Yosia nodded then stepped toward her. Suddenly, a wooden pole rose from the ground and whacked him on the forehead.

'Ah!' he cried, clutching his forehead.

Molly could see he was bleeding.

'Hang on, Yosia! I'm going to get some ice!' she said.

Molly ran up the back steps then raced into the kitchen. As she pulled at the freezer door, she thought about all the times she had taken ice-creams from the freezer. This time she took two. And a bag of ice and a tea towel.

'You can't say that!' she heard her father shout.

'I'm not saying that!' she heard her mother shout back.

Molly froze for a moment, wondering what was happening. She knew her parents' voices were coming from the loungeroom which was where they always had their serious conversations.

'I'm just saying there's obviously more going on than what we realize,' her father continued.

'I know that!' her mother snapped. 'But I share Molly's concern about Michael. He's very stressed, living in that situation. It's not fair to put a child through that.'

Molly raced back outside where she saw Yosia sitting on his pumpkin under the shade of the big trees around his hut. His hand was pressed against his forehead, and blood was seeping through his fingers. Adali was hopping up and down on his knee and squawking at such a shrill pitch, it hurt her ears.

'Let me help,' Molly said, stepping toward Yosia.

She pressed the icepack against his forehead then placed his hand over it.

'I got you a chocolate ice-cream,' she said, removing the wrapper.

Yosia laughed, but not for long, because Molly thrust the ice-cream into his mouth. The icepack soon melted, so she wrapped the tea towel around it until it went damp, then she used it to wipe the blood off Yosia's face and hand.

'You're sweet, Molly,' he said.

Adali perched on Molly's shoulder where she had a better view of her beloved Yosia. Soon, the bird was cooing; a sound that reminded Molly of her cat, Kiki, when she would purr.

'Adali is the sweet one,' Molly giggled.

Yosia slurped the ice-cream while Molly held the small block of ice to his forehead.

'I don't know how you can even think of going under the house,' she said. 'It's *so* creepy.'

'It's okay,' Yosia replied. 'It's just dusty and full of cobwebs. I really must clean it.'

'Can I ask you something?' said Molly.

'Mm?'

'Were the Jeffries still here when the Calthorpe's arrived?' Molly asked.

'No, they left about a week before,' Yosia replied.

'Did the Jeffries have children?' Molly asked.

'I don't think so,' Yosia replied.

Molly knew she did not have enough information to form an opinion. She only knew the Jeffries' sudden departure gave her a bad feeling. Maybe they were bad people who had been chased away by the owners of the mine. Or maybe they were good people who lost a fight with the mine. She had no idea really, and that made her even more curious.

'The bleeding has almost stopped now,' she said. 'But you should keep the icepack on it because there's a big lump forming and—'

'I'm fine now, Molly. Thank you,' said Yosia, standing up. 'I really must get back to sorting through those boxes. I'm fairly certain I know which ones contain the Jeffries' notes.'

'Okay,' said Molly, stepping aside.

As she watched Yosia march back up the garden toward the house, she realized just how much she wanted to read the Jeffries' notes.

3

THE PEOPLE'S MARCH

Molly dreamed she was flying.

'Hey! Watch this!' she shouted down to the mountains as her body changed from a girl to a woman, to a Goddess and then a bird.

When she awoke, she felt amazing, like she could do anything. But a moment later, she felt worried and unsettled, and she did not know why. She shuffled down the hallway to the dining table, surprised to see it covered in breakfast plates and half-eaten food. Had she slept through an entire afternoon and evening, she wondered?

'Mum!' she shrieked.

'We're in here,' her mother called out.

Molly followed her mother's voice to the loungeroom. There she saw her parents sitting on the ledge under the massive window that overlooked the mountains. But they were not looking at the mountains. They were staring down at the street.

'Is it tomorrow all ready?' Molly asked.

Her father laughed.

'Did you sleep through an entire afternoon and evening?' he asked. 'The answer is *yes*.'

Molly shuffled toward her parents, feeling confused. And when she gazed down at her street, she felt even more confused.

'Why are there so many people on our street?' she asked.

'Do you remember I was telling you about the strike at the mine?' her father asked.

'Yes,' Molly replied.

'Well, those people down there are protesting about the problems in the mine,' he explained. 'And there are many more protesting against the slurry leaching through the jungle.'

'What does *protest* mean?' Molly asked.

'Taking a stand,' her mother replied. 'Making your concern known in public.'

Molly pressed her face against the window and looked both ways.

'There must be hundreds!' she said. 'Are they also upset that Eddie was fired from his job for writing about the slurry leach?'

'Possibly,' her father replied. 'The most important thing for you to understand is that the whole thing has become a whirlwind of distress, so we think—'

'You're not leaving the house,' her mother interrupted. 'Do you understand me?'

Molly heard a tone in her mother's voice she had not heard before. It sounded a bit like anger, but slightly different.

'Are you frightened, Mum?' she asked.

Her mother took in a deep breath.

'Yes,' she said. 'I *am* frightened.'

Molly did not understand.

'But it's good that everyone is caring about the plants and animals in the jungle,' she argued.

'It is good,' her mother replied. 'But some problems get worse before they get better. In this case, your father and I think the situation might get a bit scary for a while.'

'What do you mean?' Molly asked. 'Will those people burn our house down?'

Her father laughed then shook his head.

'No, but there might be some angry people—' he started.

He stopped talking because there was a strange sound outside. To Molly's ears, it sounded like voices singing, but not singing. Or shouting, but not shouting. She looked at her parents and could tell they were also confused by the sound.

'What are they saying?' she asked.

'They're chanting,' her father replied.

'What does that mean?' Molly asked.

'It's one or two words, repeated several times,' her mother replied.

'But I don't know what words they're saying,' said Molly. 'Do you?'

Her mother shook her head slowly.

The street was suddenly so crowded, the people were piling onto the front lawns of all the houses. Some were holding big signs above their heads, but the signs were not facing Molly so she could not see what was written on them.

'Are they marching toward the mine?' she asked.

'I think so,' her father replied.

'But they can't get in, can they?' her mother asked.

'No,' said Molly's father. 'The only people with keys are the Calthorpes.'

Molly's mother stared at him.

'Should we go next door and check on Philippa?' she asked.

'I'll do that,' her father replied. 'Molly, stay here with Mum.'

'But I—'

'Stay here with Mum,' he repeated. 'I'm serious, Molly. Just stay here.'

4

CLEAN WATER, CLEAN LIVES

When Molly's father returned, his face looked longer than usual.

'What did Philippa say?' her mother asked.

'She's not there,' he replied. 'I confess, I'm quite worried about her.'

Molly's mother gave him a sad smile.

'Don't worry, darling,' she said. 'I'm sure she's just caught up with work. She'll be dealing with the union reps, the media and her boss in Brisbane.'

Molly's father sunk into a lounge chair and sighed.

'Indeed,' he said. 'And the mine was recently bought by an American company, so that could be complicating things further.'

'Hang on,' said Molly's mother. 'If Philippa's not home, where's Michael?'

'He was there alone, the poor kid, so I brought him back with me,' her father whispered. 'He headed straight toward our fridge. I think he might be stress-binging.'

A moment later, Michael wandered into the loungeroom. His face and t-shirt were covered in the dark stains of coca cola. There were crumbs on his face and t-shirt. There was even a blob of cream on his chin which, Molly suspected, was from the left-over apple pie her mother had made the previous day. She knew the boy had a habit of stuffing his face when he was stressed. But this time, he had outdone himself.

'Hey,' he murmured, wiping his mouth.

'Hey dude,' said Molly. 'Are you okay?'

'Yeah,' Michael replied, flopping onto a chair.

Molly's parents looked at the boy with worried eyes.

'When was the last time you spoke with your mum, Michael?' asked Molly's mother.

'When she dropped me off after we visited Dad at the hospital,' he replied.

Molly saw her mother's face crumple with worry.

'But that was yesterday, around lunch time,' she said.

'Yeah,' said Michael, licking his fingers.

Molly's mother sat beside Michael.

'Have you been home alone all that time?' she asked.

Michael shrugged.

'I guess so,' he said.

Molly felt her heart racing with panic. The thought of being left at home alone for that long was very upsetting. She noticed the dark shapes under Michael eyes and the food stains on his shoes. Then she looked at her parents. They glanced at each other with worried eyes.

'I'm so sorry, Michael,' said Molly's mother. 'We had no idea you were home alone. Why didn't you come and stay with us?'

Michael's face fell as though the idea was only just occurring to him for the first time.

'Um,' he said.

'Michael, please understand you have a home here with us,' she said.

'Okay,' said Michael, licking the fingers on his other hand.

Molly figured it might be a good idea to change the subject.

'How is your dad?' she asked.

'He's good, thanks,' Michael replied. 'He's well enough to come home, but the hospital is keeping him for a bit longer because he can't get up the steps of our house until his knee heals.'

'How much longer will that be?' Molly asked.

Michael's shoulders slumped.

'It should be now,' he groaned. 'We have a room for him under the house. But instead of getting it ready for him, Mum has gone to work.'

'A room under the house?' Molly echoed. 'But there are no walls underneath these houses. Only stilts.'

Michael shook his head.

'On the far side, toward the back, we have a small section that has walls,' Michael replied. 'It's a nice little room, actually. I'm not sure why we have it. No one else's house has one.'

Molly's father nodded.

'When these houses were first built, they were for the families of the Australian Army,' he said. 'The Chief Medical Officer lived in your place, and that was his little treatment center.'

'Oh,' said Michael, nodding.

'Listen, mate, I hope you know you can ask us for any help you need,' said Molly's father.

Michael's eyes watered, then he looked down at the carpet.

'Was your mum okay the last time you saw her?' Molly asked.

Michael sighed.

'I don't think so,' he replied. 'The big boss in Australia has been calling her every five minutes, yelling at her. And one of the union reps from the mine has been doing the same thing.'

'She's stuck in the middle of this problem,' said Molly's father. 'It's very tough.'

'I just hope she doesn't take off again,' said Michael.

Molly did not know what Michael meant by that and her parents looked just as confused.

'Dad's knee was injured a few years ago when a lump of iron ore fell on him,' Michael explained. 'He was in agony for a long time. He couldn't walk, but Mum didn't care. She just took off. For a year. Without a word of explanation.'

Molly felt a surge of anger toward Mrs. Calthorpe.

'Then she returned home one day as though nothing had happened,' Michael continued. 'She said she had finished her mining project in Borneo, and we all pretended everything was fine. But it wasn't fine. Dad was a mess and so was I.'

Molly tried to imagine what it would feel like if her mother or father just took off for a year, but it was impossible to imagine. She wondered if Mrs. Calthorpe had always been like that. Or perhaps she had turned strange after Michael's sister had drowned.

'I'm so sorry for what you've all been through,' said Molly's mother.

Michael grunted then stood up.

'Thanks Mrs. Marsh,' he said. 'I think I need some sunshine.'

Molly followed Michael to the back door. She watched him gazing at the sky, and she knew he was clearing his mind. But when Yosia's loud footsteps pounded up the garden, Molly and Michael looked at him, instead. With his extra-long legs, he was at the top of the steps in a moment.

'May I come in?' he asked.

'Sure!' said Molly, holding the door open for him.

She and Michael followed Yosia back into the loungeroom.

'Good afternoon, Mr. and Mrs. Marsh,' said Yosia. 'Please forgive this intrusion. I just wanted to be sure you're okay.'

Molly's mother turned away from the window and gave Yosia a sad smile.

'I'm quite worried about this chaos outside,' she said.

'It's a large crowd,' Yosia replied. 'But it won't get violent. Don't worry about that.'

'Do you know what they're chanting?' Molly's father asked.

'Clean water, clean lives,' Yosia replied.

Molly saw her father's face fall. He slumped in his chair, gripping the armrest.

'What's wrong, Dad?' she asked.

'If that's what they're chanting, it means the slurry has not only leached into the soil around the mine, but it's also made its way into the drinking water,' her father replied.

'Surely not,' Molly's mother argued. 'If that was the case, we'd be sick by now.'

Molly's father shook his head.

'We get our drinking water from the mountains,' he replied. 'But the people in the center of town get their water from a reservoir closer to the mine.'

'Oh, God,' said Molly's mother, dropping her head into her hands.

'Please grab a seat, Yosia,' said Molly's father, pouring him a glass of juice.

'Thank you, Mr. Marsh,' he said, taking the glass.

Molly could see the worry lines around Yosia's eyes and mouth.

'Did you know this was going to happen?' she asked.

'Yes,' said Yosia. 'They are very angry.'

'They have every reason to be,' said Molly's father.

'But why are they marching toward *this* end of the mine?' Molly asked. 'The entrance is so small and—'

'They don't want to enter the mine,' Yosia replied. 'They simply want their protest to be seen and heard. There are more protestors blocking the other entrances, too.'

Molly thought that was a clever plan.

Her father tapped on his phone for a moment.

'Michael, I've just sent a text to your mum to let her know you're safe with us,' he said.

'Thanks, Mr. Marsh,' said Michael.

'I can see media people down there,' said Molly's mother.

Molly raced to the window and stared down at the street. Among the tightly packed crowd she saw some people with big cameras. And someone was holding a big furry microphone above them.

'We should turn on the TV,' she said.

Molly, her parents, and Michael huddled around the TV.

'I shall leave you to it,' said Yosia, standing up.

As Molly watched Yosia leave the house, she knew he would have no need for TV news. He already knew everything there was to know, which made her wonder if he had read the Jeffries' notes yet.

5

MRS. CALTHORPE WANTS ANSWERS

A sudden knock on the back door made everyone jump. Molly's father got up to answer it.

'Philippa!' Molly heard him say. 'Please come in.'

Michael leapt out of his chair and ran to the door.

'Mum!' he shouted.

Molly and her mother scuttled after Michael and soon found themselves standing by the dining table, looking at Mrs. Calthorpe. The woman was just inside the back door. The light of the afternoon sun framed her entire body, making her look as though she might burst into flames. Her body looked smaller than usual, crumpled, perhaps.

'Philippa,' said Molly's mother, reaching toward the woman.

But Mrs. Calthorpe did not seem to understand the kindness Molly's mother was offering. Her face, almost as flat as a stone, and nearly as grey, was completely without expression. And her arms hung down by her sides like a ragdoll's.

'You're exhausted, Philippa,' said Molly's mother. 'Please sit down.'

Without a word, Mrs. Calthorpe sat down. Then she dropped her head into her hands and sighed. Michael sat beside her and wrapped his arm around her shoulders.

'Take it easy, Mum,' he said.

Mrs. Calthorpe took in a deep breath.

'The situation has become very complicated,' she said.

Molly's mother placed a jug of fruit juice and some fresh glasses in the center of the table.

'Please tell us what's going on, Philippa,' she said.

Mrs. Calthorpe cleared her throat.

'You're aware of the miners' strike, right?' she asked.

Everyone nodded.

'I can only imagine how stressful it's been,' said Molly's mother, filling the glasses.

Mrs. Calthorpe gasped, somehow making a sound like fingernails scratching a blackboard.

'Stressful barely covers it!' she said. 'I've had reporters and government officials calling me every few minutes, with one thing after another. Not to mention my boss in Brisbane.'

'Is there anything we can do to help?' asked Molly's father.

'Yes, there is,' Mrs. Calthorpe replied.

She opened her backpack and pulled out a large, clear plastic bag containing two pairs of shoes. Molly recognized them instantly. One pair was her sandals and the other was Michael's sandshoes. She remembered leaving them in the dome the previous morning.

'I want Molly and Michael to tell me what these were doing in the dome,' said Mrs. Calthorpe.

'What dome?' asked Molly's father.

Mrs. Calthorpe did not answer him. Instead, she just glared at Molly and Michael, her eyes flashing with rage.

'Where did you find them, Mrs. Calthorpe?' Molly asked, reaching for the bag.

Mrs. Calthorpe pulled the bag away from Molly's grasp and returned it to her backpack.

'Philippa, what's going on?' asked Molly's mother.

But Mrs. Calthorpe's only response was to continue glaring at Molly and Michael.

'Do you recognize the sandals as yours, Molly?' she asked.

Molly felt all the blood draining out of her face and neck. Where it was going, she did not know. She only knew it felt awful.

'Please tell us what's going on!' said Molly's mother.

'Perhaps Michael and Molly can answer that question,' Mrs. Calthorpe replied.

Molly glanced at Michael. His face was almost as white as the surface of the kitchen bench. He returned Molly's gaze for a moment then cleared his throat.

'Mum, I don't—' he started.

'Just answer the question, Michael,' Mrs. Calthorpe snapped. 'You too, Molly.'

'Philippa, you can't come in here and interrogate my daughter like this,' said Molly's mother. 'Just tell us what's going on and we'll help you any way we can.'

Mrs. Calthorpe glanced at Molly's mother then sighed.

'Your daughter and my son have broken into a top-level security site in the jungle,' she said.

Molly saw her mother's face drop. A moment later, she felt the heat of both her parents' gaze upon her. It made her feel so dizzy, she feared she might fall off her chair. She tried to swallow and breathe at the same time, which caused a blob of saliva to get stuck at the back of her mouth. It made her cough for what seemed like a long time and even when she had finished, her parents' eyes were still upon her.

'Explain yourself, Molly,' her mother demanded.

Molly looked at Michael, still unsure of what to say.

'Did you enter a building in the jungle?' her father asked.

'It wasn't a *real* building,' Molly replied.

Mrs. Calthorpe groaned.

'Did you go somewhere you should not have gone?' her father continued.

Molly nodded, her eyes filling with tears.

'When did you do this?' her father asked.

Molly knew it was only the previous morning, but she did not want to say that. If she gave that answer, she would have to explain how she and Michael had been sucked into the trunk of the magic tree, shrunk down to the size of ants, dragged under the surface of the earth by the mycelium network then flung back to the surface, inside the dome. Her parents would never believe that story, so she had to come up with something else. And fast.

'The day that Michael and I went for a walk through the jungle,' she lied.

Molly's father frowned for a moment.

'That was about four days ago,' he said.

Then he looked at Mrs. Calthorpe.

'The kids have already been disciplined over that misadventure, Philippa,' he said. 'I'm not going to hammer them over it again.'

'Hammer?' Mrs. Calthorpe exclaimed. 'Is that what you think I'm doing?'

Michael groaned then dropped his head into his hands.

Mrs. Calthorpe clenched her jaw.

'There's a lot you don't know, Oliver,' she said. 'And the kids were in terrible danger.'

'We knew that, and we were very upset about it,' said Molly's mother. 'But it's done, now.'

Mrs. Calthorpe leaned back and tapped the table, one finger at a time. It was a small action that reminded Molly of the moment Jimbo had done the same thing while sitting at Mrs. Calthorpe's dining table the previous morning. One of them had picked up the habit from the other, she decided, and that meant they had been spending a lot of time together.

Mrs. Calthorpe cleared her throat.

'About five kilometers from here is a huge sinkhole that catches the fresh water from the mountain waterfalls,' she explained. 'At the base of the sinkhole is a top-security research facility owned by Symbiotica.'

'Symbiotica,' Molly's father echoed. 'Isn't that's the American company that recently bought the Australian mining company that we work for?'

'Right,' said Mrs. Calthorpe.

'So does that mean you—' Molly's mother started.

'Yup!' said Mrs. Calthorpe. 'I'm responsible for that place, too!'

Molly's father leaned back and sighed.

'When did they plonk *that* problem on you?' he asked.

'About a week after we arrived here,' Mrs. Calthorpe replied.

'That's not fair,' said Molly's mother.

Mrs. Calthorpe's eyes reddened, but she continued.

'When someone tripped the alarm from inside the building yesterday morning, the security company called me out there,' she explained. 'That's when I found the kids' shoes.'

Molly remembered the awful screeching of the alarm when she had set it off. The sound had been terrifying. It had felt as though it was slicing through her like a hot knife.

'But Philippa, if that was yesterday morning, more than twenty-four hours ago, where have you been since then?' asked Molly's mother.

Mrs. Calthorpe glared at her.

'Is that truly your business, Margaret?' she asked.

'Actually, it *is* my business,' said Molly's mother. 'Michael has been home alone for all that time. He had no idea where you were. Neither did we. You didn't respond to any of the messages Oliver sent you. I'm sorry, but that entire picture concerns me greatly!'

To Molly's astonishment, Mrs. Calthorpe waved her mother away as though she was no more than a buzzing fly. Then she leaned forward and glared at Molly and Michael again.

'Tell me why you went back to the dome yesterday morning,' she said.

Molly looked at Michael and shook her head.

'We didn't,' Michael replied. 'We only went there once. Like Molly said.'

'Philippa, they were in the garden all morning,' said Molly's father. 'I saw them.'

'But their shoes were still wet when I found them,' said Mrs. Calthorpe.

'Maybe the sprinklers were on,' said Michael.

'How do you know about the sprinklers?' Mrs. Calthorpe asked.

Michael shrugged.

'The place is filled with plants, Mum,' he replied. 'There must be sprinklers in there.'

'Exactly what kind of place is it?' Molly's mother asked.

Mrs. Calthorpe cleared her throat again.

'It's a place where highly confidential biological research is being conducted,' she replied. 'The only reason I mention it is because our children broke in, putting themselves at risk.'

'At risk of what?' asked Molly's mother.

Mrs. Calthorpe's only response was to sigh.

'I'm sorry, Philippa, but I'm having trouble digesting this,' said Molly's mother. 'If it's such a top-security facility, how were two kids able to just wander in?'

Mrs. Calthorpe stared at Molly and Michael.

'That's one of the many questions I have for them,' she said.

Molly's parents looked at her, then at Michael, then back to Mrs. Calthorpe again.

'Let me pour another cool drink for you, Philippa,' said Molly's father.

'No, thanks,' said Mrs. Calthorpe. 'I have to go. I have a stack of other problems to deal with. Not only am I mediating the miners' strike and the media's queries about the slurry leach and the composition of that water, but I'm also answering questions from the Head of Security at Symbiotica about the security breech in the dome yesterday morning.'

Her hands started shaking and her eyes watered again.

'Could I please ask that you take care of Michael while I'm gone?' she whispered.

'Yes, of course!' said Molly's parents together.

Michael's eyes watered and his face blushed. Molly knew the boy had been through some terrible times in his family, and this was just another one. She wanted to wrap her arms around him and tell him everything was going to be okay. But she was not so sure it would be.

Mrs. Calthorpe stood up and straightened her shirt.

'I'm sorry, but I really do have to go,' she said.

As she stepped toward the back door, everyone stood up. And when she slammed the door behind her, everyone jumped. Molly listened to the woman stomp down the back steps, but her eyes were on Michael. She could see he was sweating and trembling. More than anything, she wanted to bring him down to the garden so they could feel the fresh air racing through their lungs and the sunshine warming their bones. She stepped toward him, but her father stopped her.

'You're not going outside,' he said.

He pointed to the two empty chairs opposite him.

'Sit down, you two,' he said. 'You're going to tell me everything you know.'

6

MR. MARSH WANTS ANSWERS

Molly felt the need to look at Michael before answering her father's questions, but it was difficult because her father had sat them side by side.

'I'm serious, kids,' he said. 'I want to know *everything*.'

Michael leaned forward and dropped his head into his hands.

'It's been crazy,' he groaned.

Molly's father kept his eyes on the boy, waiting for him to say more, but Molly jumped in.

'Dad, you know that I often talk about magic, right?' she started.

Her father rolled his eyes.

'Dad, if you want to know the truth, you have to let me speak!' she said.

'Fair point, muppet,' her father said. 'I'm listening.'

Molly desperately wanted to tell her parents everything she had experienced since arriving in their new home - Yosia's ability to bring the butterflies back to life, his bird-woman wife, the contaminated lake inside the volcano, the weird plants and animals down there, the cassowary chase, rolling down the mountain into the valley, taking a white flower from the vine inside the Symbiotica dome, planting in in her garden, growing a magic tree, riding the mycelium network, exploring the Symbiotica dome again and being rescued by Adali the magic bird-woman - but she knew they would never believe her. So she decided to only tell him about the Symbiotica dome.

'Okay,' she started. 'Do you remember a few days ago when—'

Yosia appeared at the back door.

'G'day, Yosia,' said Molly's father. 'Come in, mate.'

Yosia shuffled inside, carrying a carton of food. He placed it on the kitchen bench.

'Thanks, Yosia,' said Molly's mother. 'I'll deal with this.'

Yosia's eyes roamed around the kitchen table.

'Would you mind joining us, mate?' asked Molly's father. 'Molly was just about to tell us what happened in the jungle a few days ago.'

Yosia nodded, then glanced at Molly.

'Michael and I were cooling off under the waterfall at the bottom of the sinkhole,' Molly continued. 'I re-filled my water bottle and handed it to him, but it slipped through his fingers and fell into the pool of water at our feet. We watched it roll across the surface of the water and then it ... disappeared.'

Her parents' frowns deepened, so she paused.

'Go on, honey,' her mother said.

'Well, we followed it, and somehow managed to move through an invisible wall,' Molly continued. 'Suddenly we were inside this incredible dome filled with the strangest plants you've ever seen!'

Still frowning, her parents looked at Yosia. He nodded.

'It's true, Mr. and Mrs. Marsh,' he said.

'But how is that possible?' asked Molly's father.

Yosia sighed then paused. Molly knew he was thinking about the best way to explain the wall.

'It's an organic, invisible shield,' he said. 'It seems to have formed naturally as a way of protecting the natural environment from the bizarre experiments inside the Symbiotica dome.'

Molly's parents' faces went blank.

'But what do you mean when you say it's *invisible*?' asked Molly's mother.

'It seems to have the ability to manipulate light, thus making itself invisible,' Yosia replied.

'It's true!' said Michael. 'When you stand outside it, you can't see it, nor can you see what's inside it. It's like a cloaking device!'

Molly's father screwed up his face.

'Ah, come on, guys. Stop talking rub—' he started.

'Dad! You asked us to tell you!' said Molly. 'We're telling you the truth!'

Her father sighed loudly then looked at her mother. She looked at Yosia.

'Were you with the kids when they made this discovery?' she asked.

Yosia shook his head.

'No, I only retrieved them,' he replied. 'You will remember I walked them home that evening.'

'How did you know they were there?' asked Molly's mother.

Yosia shifted around in his chair. Molly could tell he was uncomfortable because he did not know how to answer the question. He did not want to admit that Adali had told him where they were. He would have to think quickly, she knew, to provide an acceptable answer.

'I know the land very well, Mrs. Marsh,' he replied. 'It was a lucky guess.'

Molly's mother nodded slightly then stared at Molly.

'So, it was about four days ago when you two had that adventure,' she said. 'Why then, would your shoes have still been wet when Mrs. Calthorpe found them yesterday?'

'I'm sure the sprinklers switch on every morning, Mum,' said Molly.

But her mother continued to glare at her.

'Were you kids in the dome yesterday as well?' she asked.

Molly felt a hard lump forming in her throat, so she was relieved when her father intervened.

'Darling, I told you I saw them in the garden yesterday morning,' he said.

Molly's mother glared at Yosia again.

'We take the kids' safety very seriously,' she said.

'As do I, Mrs. Marsh,' said Yosia. 'It's for that reason I rescued the kids from the dome and brought them home to you.'

'Fair enough, mate,' said Molly's father. 'But could you please explain this invisible wall? I mean, if it's encasing a top-security research facility, as Philippa said, how did any of you just walk through it?'

'Very few people can,' Yosia replied. 'From what I've observed, the wall resists entrance to most people. The scientists who work in the dome have to cut their way through with lasers.'

Molly felt a sharp pain her chest as she imagined the

wall being cut by a laser. Her eyes started to burn with tears.

'Are you okay, honey?' her mother asked.

Everyone looked at Molly.

'It's very upsetting to think of a living organism being cut with a laser,' she gasped.

Yosia nodded.

'It's horrible,' he agreed. 'But somehow, those cuts seal within seconds.'

Molly's father frowned again.

'How long have you known about this place, Yosia?' he asked.

'A few months,' Yosia replied.

'How did you find out about it?' asked Molly's mother.

'One evening, close to sunset, I was walking home through the valley,' Yosia explained. 'I stopped for a rest at the edge of the sinkhole. Although I was staring down at the bottom of the hole, I couldn't see the dome because of the invisible shield around it. But when Adali flew down there and suddenly disappeared, I knew there was something strange down there.'

'Did you tell anyone?' Molly's father asked.

'No,' said Yosia.

'Were the Jeffries living here at the time?' Molly's father continued.

'Yes, but I didn't mention it to them because we rarely spoke about anything,' Yosia replied. 'They seemed like very private people. They didn't socialize with anyone, and they never seemed interesting in speaking with me about anything.'

'Do you think the Jeffries knew about this invisible dome?' asked Molly's mother.

Yosia's eyebrows raised so high, Molly thought they were going to disappear into his hair.

'I have been wondering that,' he replied. 'I guess we'll know when we read their notes.'

'Speaking of which,' said Molly's father. 'Have you made progress retrieving them from the boxes under the house?'

'I have,' Yosia replied. 'May I bring them to you?'

'Yes, please,' said Molly's father.

As Yosia stepped out of the back door, Molly's parents looked at each other.

'Please don't blame Yosia,' Molly whispered.

'We're not, muppet,' her father replied, clutching her hand. 'We're just trying to put the pieces of the puzzle together.'

'While keeping you safe,' her mother added.

Molly felt terrible that Yosia had been put under pressure by her parents, but she was pleased to have learned a few more things about the dome. She glanced at Michael. His face seemed to have brightened.

Her father let out a loud groan then scratched his head.

'This is all *way* above my pay grade,' he said.

'It might be above Philippa's pay grade, too,' said Molly's mother.

Michael grunted.

'Whatever they're up to in that place, it must be more complicated than anything Mum has dealt with before,' he said. 'I've never seen her as stressed as she is now. She's even been shouting and crying in her sleep!'

'Ah, poor Philippa,' said Molly's mother.

Michael grunted again, then his eyes filled with tears.

7
MOLLY AND MICHAEL WANT ANSWERS

Molly saw her parents huddled around the dining table reading the Jeffries' notes. Although she was curious about the contents, she knew her parents wanted to read them first, so she would have to wait until tomorrow to find out more.

She stepped outside and lay on her picnic blanket between Michael and Yosia. Staring at the half-moon enveloped by the deep indigo sky, she noticed the stars were starting to twinkle.

'We never see this many in Sydney!' she said.

'Nor in Melbourne,' Michael added.

Molly pictured the furry black face and green eyes of her beloved cat, Kiki. She remembered the sound of the cat's purr and she desperately wished the little snuggle pot was beside her now.

'What's wrong?' Michael asked.

'I miss my cat *so much*,' she cried.

'Ah, don't get me started,' said Michael. 'I miss Bozo so bad, it's unreal. That dog is the best friend a bloke could ever have. I wish I could go home to him right now.'

'I know what you mean,' said Molly.

For a moment, the only sound she heard was Adali cooing as Yosia stroked her.

'I miss Ted, too,' she added. 'I know that's weird because he's a lizard.'

'Poor Ted,' said Michael. 'I hope he's okay inside the volcano.'

'He's not *always* inside the volcano,' Yosia said.

Molly and Michael sat up.

'What do you know about Ted?' Molly asked.

'Gideon saw him a few days ago,' Yosia replied. 'Apparently the lizard was manic.'

'What does that mean?' Molly asked.

'Demented,' said Michael.

'What does *demented* mean?' Molly asked.

'Apparently Ted was racing through the crops hissing at nothing,' Yosia replied. 'When Gideon approached him, the beast stood up on his back legs, showed his claws and hissed even louder.'

'Any chemical that turns brown eyes to fluorescent blue would probably send a person mad,' said Michael. 'Or a lizard, for that matter.'

Molly remembered the night she had opened the laundry door and seen Ted's bright blue eyes glowing in the dark. She had been terrified, not only because they had looked so strange, but because she had sensed a mad energy from the lizard.

'That was a week ago,' she whispered. 'But it feels like a lifetime ago. So much has happened since then.'

'Yeah, and we still haven't told Yosia what happened yesterday,' said Michael.

'What happened today?' Yosia asked.

Molly hesitated, aware that Yosia had already been drilled by her parents, thanks to the trouble she had got herself into during the last few days.

'I don't think we should burden Yosia any further,' she said.

'Perhaps you could let Yosia decide for himself,' said Yosia.

Molly laughed. Then she sighed.

'Do you really want to know what we got up to yesterday?' she asked.

'You may as well tell me,' Yosia replied. 'Nothing you tell me will surprise me. And to be honest, it's been helpful to have these discussions with you both.'

'How so?' Michael asked.

'Since Adali and I became aware of the Symbiotica dome and its experiments, we've been deeply concerned,' Yosia replied. 'Your experiences have helped us to form a few theories.'

'Like what?' Molly asked.

'Mostly, we're getting a broad sense of Symbiotica's intentions,' Yosia replied. 'The strange plants and animals they've created, the slurry leach and the contaminated lakes inside the mine and the volcano are all forming a bigger picture.'

'It all points to agromining, doesn't it?' said Molly.

'I'm sure their research includes agromining,' Yosia replied. 'But we sense that is only part of their plan. There is something much bigger going on.'

'There *has* to be,' said Michael. 'I mean, no one creates dinosaurs inside volcanoes as part of improving their mining practice.'

Molly laughed.

'No, they don't,' Yosia agreed. 'But every piece of

intel we gather will help us understand what they are up to and how we can stop them from causing further harm to our ecosystem.'

Molly thought again about her parents inside, reading through the Jeffries' notes. And she wondered if the notes might include something about the dinosaurs inside the volcano.

'In the meantime, just tell me what you two got up to yesterday,' said Yosia.

Molly told Yosia everything - her visit to Michael's place where she had seen Jimbo and Mrs. Calthorpe at the kitchen table, followed by the moment she and Michael had been sucked through the hole in the magic tree, shrunk down to the size of ants, dragged underground by the mycelium network, flung to the surface inside the dome where she had set off the alarm and they had run for their lives but got stuck inside the wall.

'We had to call upon Adali to rescue us,' said Michael.

Yosia stared at them for a moment.

'Your mothers were right,' he said. 'You *were* in the dome again yesterday morning.'

'Well, yeah,' said Molly. 'But we couldn't exactly tell them *that* story now, could we?'

Yosia groaned and rubbed his brow.

'The sooner you two realize that your parents are not stupid, the better,' he said. 'They know you're not telling them the whole truth so unless you want to tell them everything, you will have to come up with some better explanations for what you've been up to.'

Then he sat up and wrapped his hands around Adali.

'Why didn't you tell me you rescued them?' he asked.

Adali chirped for longer than usual.

'What did she say?' Molly asked.

'She said she was planning to tell me, but I've been distracted,' Yosia replied. 'Which is true.'

Then he scowled at Molly and Michael.

'Do you remember I told you not to mess with the shield around the magic tree?' he asked.

'Yes, but it was not our intention to go that far,' Molly replied. 'We only wanted to touch the tree, not disappear inside it!'

'Yeah,' said Michael. 'But the good thing about that weird adventure is that we now know for sure all these things are connected. The invisible wall around the Symbiotica dome, the shield around the magic tree and the gel inside the mycelium network are all part of a single organism, aren't they?'

'Yes,' Yosia replied.

'And that organism can slow time, can't it?' Molly asked.

'Yes,' said Yosia, stroking Adali.

'And Adali is the key to all of this, isn't she?' said Molly.

Yosia hesitated for a moment.

'The organism was already in existence,' he replied. 'Adali helped it grow, that's all.'

'Why did she do that?' asked Molly.

'To help the organism create a barrier between the natural environment and Symbiotica's strange experiments,' Yosia replied.

'I'm curious,' said Michael. 'What does Symbiotica think about the invisible wall around the dome? I mean, how do they make sense of it?'

'They don't understand it,' Yosia replied. 'They seem

to think of it as nothing more than a weed, or an obstacle to their precious experiments.'

Molly had so many questions about the organism, but she wanted to ask Adaline the human, not Adali the bird. It would be much easier to speak with a human than have Yosia translate every little chirp from the bird. She was just about to suggest that when she remembered Michael did not yet know that Adali the bird and Adaline the woman were the same being. Yosia had told her to keep that secret to herself because he believed Michael should see the transformation for himself. And only when he was ready. Molly knew she was starting to lose track of who knew what, and it was exhausting her. She just wanted everyone to know everything because it would make her life a lot easier.

'Yosia, can you tell us how the network shrunk us?' Michael asked.

'It has the ability to shrink the space between atoms,' Yosia replied.

'No way!' said Michael. 'That only happens in comic books!'

'I don't know what a comic book is,' said Yosia.

'What else can it do?' Molly asked.

'Condense time,' Yosia replied.

Michael's eyes were bulging.

'That's what you said *you* did when you brought the butterflies back to life!' he said.

'Not exactly,' said Yosia. 'I said I brought together two different versions of space-time.'

Molly tried to understand the difference, but she knew it was beyond her.

'I've only been able to do that since Adali helped the

organism grow these shields,' Yosia continued. 'Somehow, I can tap into its frequency.'

'Is that because of your connection with Adali?' Molly asked.

'I think so,' Yosia replied.

'So, when Michael and I moved through the invisible wall around the Symbiotica dome, were we doing something similar?' Molly asked.

Yosia shook his head.

'The organism merely sensed your goodness and decided to let you in,' he replied.

'But why did it let us through the first time, only to hold us hostage the second time?' Michael asked.

'Hostage?' Yosia echoed.

'Yes,' said Molly. 'It held us inside the wall. Like flies in a spider's web, we were trapped. That's why we had to call upon Adali for help.'

Yosia and Adali exchanged glances then Adali chirped again.

'What did she say?' asked Molly.

'She said the organism held you inside its wall to protect you from the guards and their dogs,' Yosia replied.

'Wow,' said Molly. 'That's incredible.'

'How did the guards and dogs enter the dome?' Michael asked.

'They would have used their lasers to cut through as they always do,' said Yosia.

Molly lay back on the grass and stared at the night sky, feeling the need to soothe her mind and process all this new, incredible information. The inside of her head felt like a washing machine on the spin cycle, and she wanted it to stop.

Michael yawned.

'I need to sleep,' he said.

'Me too,' said Molly. 'Let's go inside. Mum has made up the sofa for you.'

Yosia stood up and stretched, then Adali landed on his wild mop of curly hair.

'Ha-ha!' said Molly. 'It looks like your hair has grown a beak.'

Yosia laughed.

'Sleep well, kids,' he said.

'You too, Yosia.'

8

THE JEFFRIES' NOTES

Molly was surprised by the brightness in her bedroom when she woke. And even more surprised to see that her bedside clock showed the time as 9:47 a.m.

'Oh, no,' she gasped, sitting bolt upright.

She felt certain she was running late for something. But for what, she did not know.

'Mum!' she shouted.

She heard footsteps down the hallway. A moment later, her mother appeared at the door of her bedroom. Her hair was tied back in a high ponytail, and she was wearing her reading glasses.

'Good morning, sleepyhead,' she said, approaching Molly's bed.

'What happened?' Molly asked.

'Nothing happened, honey,' her mother replied. 'You slept in, that's all.'

'But I—'

'Don't panic,' said her mother. 'You obviously needed the rest.'

Molly threw her Wonder Woman bedsheet aside and

struggled out of bed. Then she stood in the middle of her bedroom, staring out of the window. The sky was bright blue, and the tops of the hibiscus trees were shining under the sunlight.

'I can't believe it's so late!' she said.

'You're getting older. You can expect a few changes,' her mother explained. 'There's nothing to be worried about.'

'Is everyone okay?' Molly asked.

'Of course, honey. The protesters have gone, so the street is quiet again,' her mother replied. 'Michael and Yosia are at the dining table with your father. We're going through the Jeffries' notes so if that's of interest to you, th —'

'Thanks, Mum,' said Molly, dashing down the hallway.

When she reached the dining table, she saw everyone crowded around a pile of papers. Crumpled and stained, the papers looked even more intriguing than she had imagined.

'So what have we learned?' she asked, blinking.

'We're starting to piece it all together, muppet,' her father replied. 'The Jeffries made a record of several concerns about the operations of the mine.'

'Like what?' Molly asked.

'The mine's failure to reduce the seismic activity caused by the trucks and excavation of the ore,' he replied, clutching several sheets of paper.

'And here, too, Mr. Marsh, they talk about the chemical analysis of the slurry,' Michael added.

'Not to mention the systemic bullying and harassment of laborers,' said Yosia.

'What does that mean?' Molly asked.

'Whenever a worker expressed a concern about anything, they were bullied,' Yosia explained.

'That's horrible,' said Molly.

'Hey, listen to this!' said Michael. 'Reports of contaminated slurry leaching beyond the perimeter of the mine site and surfacing elsewhere.'

He looked at Molly.

'We certainly know about that, don't we?' he scoffed. 'So does Ted.'

Molly's mother frowned at Michael.

'Ted?' she echoed. 'Wasn't that the name for the big lizard in our garden?'

Michael suddenly looked as though he realized he had said too much.

'I haven't seen that beast for almost a week,' Molly's mother continued. 'Where did he go?'

Molly glared at Michael, wondering how he could have been stupid enough to almost tell her parents they had witnessed Ted falling into the contaminated lake inside the volcano.

'Hey, muppet, listen to this,' said Molly's father. 'The Jeffries talk about genetic engineering of local plants in an unknown location away from the mine site.'

'Well, that's got to be the dome,' said Michael.

Molly's father nodded.

'They go on to question if the mine is experimenting with agromining,' he said.

'I was right!' said Molly.

Her father frowned.

'How so?' he asked.

'Seriously, Dad, it's a real thing!' Molly insisted. 'It's about using plants to suck the metals out of the rocks instead of going underground to extract them.'

Her father laughed.

'I know what agromining is,' he said. 'I'm a mining engineer, remember? I'm just surprised that you've heard about it. It's a new concept, with very little practical application so far.'

'I know, but—'

'How did you hear about it?' Michael asked.

Molly leaned toward him.

'Remember the other day, during our walk through the plantation, you told me it looked like an agroforestry project?' she asked.

Michael nodded.

'Well, I researched that when I got home,' said Molly. 'And that's when I found agromining.'

'That's it,' her father said. 'I'm blocking you from our internet connection.'

'What!' Molly shouted, standing up.

'Calm down, honey, your father was only joking,' her mother said.

'I am joking, muppet,' her father agreed. 'But don't get ahead of yourself, okay?'

'With respect, Mr. Marsh,' said Yosia. 'I think Molly might be onto something.'

'I *am* onto something!' Molly insisted. 'And I've just remembered the word for the plants they use in agromining. They're called *hyperaccumulators* because they accumulate the metal.'

'That's correct, muppet,' her father replied. 'But, as I said before, that research is new. It's been tested around nickel mines. As you know, we are mining copper here.'

'I know,' said Molly. 'But I reckon Symbiotica is engineering new plants that have never existed before just to see if they can accumulate the copper.'

Molly desperately wanted to ask her father if the Jeffries had written anything about the dinosaurs living in the jungle inside the volcano. But she did not dare.

'Do they say anything about animal experiments?' she asked.

Her father shook his head.

'You know what I think?' said Molly, eating a piece of cold pancake from her mother's plate.

'What's that?' her father replied without looking at her.

'I think Michael and I have spent the last twenty-four hours sitting around the house, talking,' said Molly. 'It's boring! We need to get some fresh air!'

Molly's parents looked at each other. She knew they were trying to decide how they felt about her going out.

Her mother sighed.

'I guess that's okay,' she said. 'The protestors have gone so it should be safe.'

Her father nodded.

'You can go for a walk, but only if Yosia is available to join you,' he said.

Everyone looked at Yosia. Then he looked at Molly's mother.

'Do you need me for anything today, Mrs. Marsh?' he asked.

'No, thank you, Yosia,' she replied. 'But please don't feel obliged to hang out with the kids.'

Everyone looked at each other. Molly figured they were all uncertain about what they should do with the day ahead. She could not tolerate the indecision anymore. Before she knew it, she had slapped the surface of the table and was standing up.

'Well, I'm going outside!' she said. 'Michael and

Yosia, I'd like you to come with me. Dad, I think you should get those notes in chronological order so we can make better sense of them.'

Molly's mother glared at her.

'Do you have any instructions for me, mon capitaine?'

Everyone laughed.

'Sorry, I don't mean to be bossy,' said Molly. 'I'm just desperate for fresh air and sunshine.'

A moment later, she was halfway down the back steps. As her feet landed on the grass, she looked up, pleased to see Michael and Yosia were descending, too.

'Yosia, there's something I've always wanted to know,' she said.

'What could that possibly be?' asked Yosia, smiling at her.

'What's behind your hut?' Molly asked.

She knew it was a cheeky question, so she was not surprised when Yosia took a step back. His eyebrows lifted, and a small smile moved across his face.

'You're in quite a mood today,' he said.

Molly knew she was, and she did not have an explanation for her impatience.

'I've always been curious,' she said. 'As far as I can tell, there are several tall trees behind your hut, but they seem quite far back, which means there must be a little clearing behind your hut. What's it for?'

Yosia laughed.

'In all my years of living here, no one has ever made that observation,' he said. 'And no one has ever been cheeky enough to invade my privacy with a question like that.'

Michael shook his head.

'Cheeky is Molly's middle name,' he said.

Yosia laughed.

'Do you really want to know what's behind my hut?' he asked.

'Yes,' said Molly.

'Fine,' he said. 'Follow me.'

The instant they stepped around the side of Yosia's hut, Molly felt her skin prickle with excitement. Whatever she was about see, she knew it was going to be awesome. But when they arrived, she wondered why she had been so thrilled.

'Oh,' she said, staring at the clearing.

The ground was grey which, she knew, was the result of years of ash from the little fire in the center of the clearing. Around the perimeter were five seats made from pieces of bamboo that had been bound together in an artful manner.

'I think my dad would call this *fine craftsmanship*,' said Molly.

'Well, thank you for the compliment, Molly,' Yosia replied. 'It took a while to make them.'

'You're good with wood, Yosia,' said Michael, pulling on the leather strap around his neck.

A moment later, he was holding the beautiful wooden carving of Adali that Yosia had made.

'I'm glad you like it,' said Yosia.

'Do you have parties here?' Molly asked.

'I used to,' Yosia replied. 'In my youth.'

Molly looked at the wrinkles on Yosia's throat.

'How long ago was that?' she asked.

Yosia sighed.

'Gosh, you really are a cheeky little thing,' he replied.

Michael scowled at Molly.

'Even I know better than to ask questions like that,' he said.

Molly knew she was out of line but there was an impatience burning within her, and it was making her feel restless.

'I don't mean to be rude,' she explained. 'There are just so many things I want to know.'

Yosia stepped to the far side of the clearing then sat in one of his beautiful chairs. A swooshing sound swept through the air then Adali landed on his shoulder.

'Is it time to show them, my love?' he asked.

Adali chirped.

'What are you going to show us?' asked Molly.

Yosia and Adali exchanged glances again.

'Last night, Adali and I were talking about you two,' said Yosia. 'We were commenting on how impressed we are by your understanding of the natural world.'

Adali chirped for longer than usual. Yosia nodded.

'We know you still have many more questions, and we're happy to answer them,' he said. 'But for now, we thought it might be helpful to show you.'

'Show us what?' Michael asked.

'Adali's birthplace,' Yosia replied.

Molly felt her skin prickle with goosebumps.

'That would be awesome,' she whispered.

'Is it walking distance from here?' Michael asked. 'Will we be back in time for lunch?'

Yosia laughed.

'It's definitely *not* walking distance,' he replied. 'But you *will* be home for lunch.'

A confused frown creeped across Michael's face, but Molly felt excited. She knew something strange and magical was about to happen.

'We're going to fly there,' said Yosia, smiling.

Molly gasped with joy.

'Can you guess how we're going to do that?' Yosia asked.

'No,' said Michael. 'I wish you'd just tell me what you're talking about.'

'Yes, please just tell us!' Molly squealed, clasping her hands together.

'Adali is going to fly us there,' said Yosia.

'What?' Michael scoffed.

'She can shrink us, can't she?' said Molly.

Yosia nodded, slowly gazing from Molly to Michael.

Michael leaned back so far, Molly thought he might fall to the ground.

'I'm not sure I want to be shrunk again,' he said, his voice wavering.

'You don't have to, but I'm going to!' said Molly, jumping to her feet.

Michael held up his hand.

'Hang on,' he said. 'If Adali shrinks us, she'll condense time, too, won't she?'

'Yes,' said Yosia.

'Okay,' said Michael. 'Does that mean we might return before we leave?'

Molly burst out laughing.

'Not usually,' Yosia replied.

'What do you mean by that?' asked Michael.

'On a few occasions we have noticed a very slight variance in time or space upon returning,' Yosia replied. 'But it's so slight, we never worry about it. As I said before, you don't have to do this.'

'I do!' said Molly. 'Let's go!'

Michael did not look pleased.

'You stay here, then,' she said.

Michael groaned.

'Ah, I may as well do it,' he said.

Yosia nodded at them both.

'Let's get ready,' he said, waving Molly and Michael toward him. 'Stand on either side of me.'

Molly and Michael did as he said. A moment later, Molly heard the fluttering of Adali's wings above them. Soon, she saw a soft white glow around herself, Michael and Yosia. A moment later, the glow became more solid, like the semi-transparent shield she had seen around the magic tree and inside the wall around the Symbiotica dome.

'Oh, wow,' she heard Michael say, his voice sounding deeper, slower, and further away.

A moment later, the white glow became so bright, Molly had to close her eyes. And when she opened them, she did not recognize where she was. She could no longer see Yosia's long brown limbs, nor could she feel his shoulder under the palm of her hand.

'Where am I?' she asked.

Beside her was the trunk of a huge old tree. It was so high, she had to tilt her head way back to see the top of it. There were no leaves, so she saw the sky beyond it, and it was as blue as ever. She heard Michael laugh, but she could not see him. Then he appeared, around the corner of the tree, with Yosia following.

'I can't believe it! Michael shrieked.

'Where are we?' Molly squealed.

'Exactly where we were before,' Yosia replied. 'We haven't left, yet.'

Molly pressed her hand into the tree trunk.

'Is this the bamboo chair we were standing next to a moment ago?' she asked.

'Yup!' said Michael.

'Where's Adali?' asked Molly.

'Right behind you,' Michael laughed.

When Molly turned around, she saw a long red-brown thing lying across the ground. It looked like one of the huge pipes that pumped water through the rural towns in Australia.

'What's that?' she asked.

'It's one of Adali's feet!' Michael shouted.

'That's our ride!' said Yosia.

Molly watched Yosia approach Adali's foot. It was almost as high as his head, but he reached up, pressed his hands upon it and pull himself up.

'Come on, you two!' he shouted.

Molly ran toward him with her arms outstretched. Yosia grabbed her hands and pulled her up, but Michael ran to the end of Adali's claw and climbed the gentle incline until he reached the top of the bird's foot.

'I can't believe this is happening!' he laughed.

'Me neither!' said Molly. 'What next?'

'Follow me,' said Yosia.

Soon the three friends were huddled around the base of Adali's leg.

'Lean back!' Yosia shouted.

Molly and Michael did as he said. A moment later, Molly saw the familiar burst of white light from Adali's body. It encased her, Michael and Yosia, holding them in place and keeping them safe.

'Are we invisible to the outside world now?' she heard herself say more slowly than usual.

'Yes,' Yosia replied, sounding just as slow.

But the shield Adali had created around them was just as transparent as the one around the Symbiotica dome, so Molly could see everything around her. *This is going to be awesome*, she thought. And she was right. The scenery changed fast. No longer was she surrounded by bamboo furniture, but open space, treetops, and blue sky. And this was only the beginning.

9

THE MOST INCREDIBLE FLIGHT

Molly had always loved to fly, but this was something else.

'Yee-ha!' she screamed. 'This is awesome!'

In Michael's face she could see excitement and terror in equal parts.

'Don't worry, we're in safe hands!' she shouted.

To her left, Molly could see a deep blue ocean. Beyond it, she knew, would be the northern tip of Queensland. In an instant her mind became flooded with memories of a holiday she'd had on Thursday Island just north of the tip. The scraggly, wind-swept trees and the jade green ocean had been a stark contrast against the black rocks.

Her father had been fascinated by the Green Hill Fort and the role it had played in keeping Australia safe from Japanese and Russian attacks at various times in history. But Molly and her mother had found the Cultural Festival far more interesting, especially the Islanders' colorful costumes and dances. It had been the first time Molly had felt the sound of drums banging through her chest so ferociously, she had been compelled to dance.

But now she listened to the beating of Adali's wings. Steady, rhythmic, and unchanging, the sound made her feel happy and safe. She tilted her head back and gazed at the pale brown feathers covering the bird's belly. It looked so soft and warm in there, Molly wondered if Adali had even been a mother. Then she peered at the view across the far side of the bird's leg and saw the long tail of Papua New Guinea. A deep green color, thanks to its thick jungle, the land looked more enticing and mysterious than ever before. And as they traveled further north, the jungle became even thicker and darker.

'We're headed for the center, aren't we?' Molly shouted.

But the wind took her voice in the opposite direction, so no one heard her. She could see Yosia's eyes were fixed on a north-easterly point which, she knew, was the center of the country. *We're going to Mount Giluwe*, she told herself. Soon she saw the massive brown rock that was its famous volcanic mountain. And when Adali flew lower, Molly knew she was looking at thousands of species of trees, ferns, orchids, moss, and lichen. For a moment, she wanted to be down there exploring, but Mount Giluwe was soon behind her.

As Adali continued further northwest, Molly stretched her memory in search of anything she might have learned about this part of the country. *Enga Province* was the name that came to her mind. She remembered learning that its landscape was one of the most wild and rugged in the country. Flying over it now, Molly felt certain it was even more mysterious than the parts of the country she had already seen. Through the expanse of green, she could see some thin brown lines. Farming, she knew.

Next, Molly caught a glimpse of an oval-shaped lake surrounded by lush jungle. She ran her fingertips across the surface of Adali's leg, noticing the softness and moveability of the bird's flesh. And she wondered, for the hundredth time, how Adali got along with other birds. What would happen if Adali landed on a lake among other birds, she wondered. Would they accept her, fear her, or attack her? Or would she make herself invisible to them? Molly's mind whirled with so many questions, she had to force them away to continue enjoying the view.

She glanced at Michael. He gave her a weak smile, but when Adali headed downward, all the color left the boy's face in an instant. But Molly did not feel afraid. Not for a second. She leaned back and pressed her body against Adali's leg and took in a deep breath. Then she turned toward Yosia just as Adali dive-bombed downward. The descent was so sudden and steep, Molly felt a surge of panic shoot through her veins. Below she saw the shapes of the treetops, far too clearly. A moment later, they blurred, as though she was looking at them through a dirty lens. Next, the blur became a flash of bright white light obscuring her view of everything around her. She heard a *bang!* and a moment later, she was somewhere else.

The sky was a warm pink color - paler above and deeper at the horizon line. Directly below was a muddy brown lake, perfectly circular in shape. Its surface was still, and it was surrounded by a neat circle of brown, cone-shaped stones. Molly had never seen anything like this. When she looked at Michael, she almost laughed out loud because his eyes were wide open, his mouth was gaping, and his hair was standing at a right angle to his head. Yosia looked calm and happy. He sighed gently, like someone who had returned home after a long journey, then he gazed at Molly and winked.

Adali's wings were no longer beating. She was gliding. The smooth sensation reminded Molly of the time she and her father had gone hang gliding over the Blue Mountains in Australia. But this time, she was gliding over a landscape completely unfamiliar to her. She could see the entire lake, despite her tiny form. It was a muddy brown colour, reflecting the color of the cone-shaped stones that surrounded it. And she noticed a hint of pink in the water and stones, reflecting the warm pink sky. Adali cruised down to the nearest stone, landed on its peak then folded her wings.

10

THE MAGIC REALM

Within a second of landing, Adali released the shield around Molly, Michael and Yosia. As Molly stretched and gazed around, she could hardly believe she was standing in this beautiful and serene place. It was like nothing she had ever seen before.

'I'm speechless,' she whispered.

'No, you're not,' Michael quipped.

'Are we inside another dome?' Molly asked.

'Yes,' said Adali, without opening her beak.

Molly thought she must have imagined hearing Adali, so she looked at Yosia, hoping he might explain. But he just nodded.

'She's speaking to us with her thoughts,' said Michael. 'Just as she did when we were trapped inside the wall around the dome.'

'That's right,' Yosia agreed. 'Adali can project her thoughts from inside these shields.'

'Incredible,' said Molly. 'Is our sense of time altered while we're in here?'

'Yes,' said Adali. 'You will experience time differently in this place.'

Adali sat down and stretched her red-brown legs in front of her body. Molly sat beside her and leaned against the side of her leg, enjoying the warmth and the softness of her feathers. She wrapped her hands around one of the feathers and pressed it against her face.

'It's *so* soft,' she whispered.

Then she looked up at Adali's face.

'You're even more amazing than Big Bird,' she said.

'Who is that?' Adali asked.

Michael groaned.

'Don't listen to her,' he said. 'She's talking about Big Bird from Sesame Street.'

'Sesame Street?' Yosia echoed. 'I don't know that one. Is it close to our street?'

Molly burst out laughing.

Michael just shook his head then looked up at Adali.

'Adali, may I ask you a question?' he asked.

'Anything,' Adali replied.

'We know these domes and the mycelium network belong to a single organism, so I've been wondering if there is a collective name for it,' said Michael.

'We just call it the network,' Adali replied.

'How does it work?' asked Molly.

'It transmits chemical information from one plant to another, informing them of the nutrients in their surrounding area and warning them of any threats to their ecosystem,' Adali explained.

'How did you help it grow?' Michael asked.

'It grows by itself,' said Adali. 'But when it asked for my protection, I used my magic to create the shields around it.'

'But how?' Michael asked.

'You would call it *electromagnetism*,' Adali replied.

'Okay, so electromagnetic forces occur at the atomic level, as an interaction between the nucleus of an atom and its surrounding electrons,' said Michael. 'I know that much, but I don't under—'

'You're on the right track, Michael,' Yosia interrupted. 'The only other thing you need to know is that the network can shrink the space between atoms, reducing us to the size we are now.'

'Wow,' said Michael.

'This is so weird,' Molly added.

'But how does the network slow down time?' asked Michael.

'Electromagnetic energy causes a curvature in space-time,' Yosia explained. 'Therefore, when Adali helped the network to create these shields, she changed space *and* time.'

'Gosh,' said Molly, trying to understand.

She looked up at Adali's face but could only see the underside of her beak.

'Does it hurt when you make those shields?' she asked.

'No,' Adali replied. 'It is as natural to me as building a house is to you.'

'Wow,' said Molly. 'Did you do it to protect the natural plants?'

'The plants *and* animals,' Adali replied. 'But there is more to the story.'

Yosia patted Adali's leg.

'Tell them, my love,' he said.

'The network is not only the transporter of chemical information between plants,' said Adali. 'It is also the primary mode of communication between the guardians of this land.'

Molly remembered Adaline had once said something about being a guardian of the land.

'What *exactly* does that mean?' she asked.

'There are seven guardians of this land,' Adali replied. 'Five are on the mainland and two are caring for the islands.'

'But—' Michael started.

'I have an idea,' Yosia interrupted.

He looked up at Adali.

'Just show them, my love,' he said.

Adali nodded. A moment later, the deep pink and brown colors from the horizon line crept up the sky, slowly shrouding the entire dome in darkness.

'What's happening?' Michael shrieked.

'It's okay,' said Yosia. 'Just keep your eyes on the lake.'

Molly watched the surface of the lake slowly transform into something that looked like a gigantic plasma TV screen. A blue ball broke through the surface and hovered in front of her. On the surface of the ball was a green shape that broke into three sections. The sections moved away from each other then broke into smaller sections. When they all stopped moving, Molly recognized two of the green shapes as Australia and Papua New Guinea.

'Oh, wow,' she whispered. 'From Pangaea to now.'

The ball turned then grew larger, showing only the shape that looked like Papua New Guinea. On the surface of that green shape, Molly saw some tiny green swirls. They formed little green balls that broke from the surface then travelled away from each other.

Slowly the image faded, and the sky began to brighten again.

'That was incredible!' said Michael.

'Are you one of those green balls that broke from the surface of PNG?' Molly asked.

'Yes,' Adali replied. 'I am one of the seven guardians of this land.'

'Are the other six guardians bird-people like you?' Molly asked.

'Bird-people?' Michael echoed. 'What the heck does that mean?'

Adali gazed at Michael.

'I am also Adaline, the woman you have previously met,' she said. 'I thought you knew.'

Michael leaned back, then his entire body went rigid, like one of the massive stones around the lake. Molly knew he was trying to understand, so she decided to help.

'At midnight, Adali the bird transforms into Adaline the woman,' she explained. 'Then at dawn, she transforms back to Adali the bird.'

At first, Michael did not show any sign of having heard Molly. A moment later he stared at her, his face as blank as a sheet of paper. Then he glanced at Yosia, then at the lake, then he stood up and walked away.

'Where are you going?' Molly called out.

'Leave him,' said Yosia.

Michael sat down, with his back to everyone, but close enough to hear the discussion.

Adali continued her explanation.

'None of the others share the form of a bird,' she replied. 'One is a tree kangaroo, another is a wallaby, we also have a tree frog, a fruit bat, a crocodile and a rainbowfish.'

'Wow,' said Molly. 'You've got it all covered - land, air and water.'

'Yes.'

'Do you seven communicate with each other through the network?' Molly asked.

'Yes,' said Adali.

Michael looked over his shoulder at Adali.

'That doesn't seem likely,' he scoffed. 'I mean, it's not as though fish and birds speak the same language.'

Molly felt her heart pound with embarrassment over Michael's rudeness, so she was relieved when Yosia decided to ignore it.

'Each of these guardians commune with the network through thought,' Yosia explained. 'Those thoughts are converted to biochemical information that travels, instantly, to all parts of the network.'

Molly remembered feeling the thoughts of the mycelium network. Even though she had known it was a vast network comprised of many parts, she had felt as though she was in the presence of a single entity. She looked up at Adali, again.

'Did you create the network?' she asked.

'No, it existed long before me and it will continue forever,' Adali replied.

'For how long have you, and the other six guardians, been alive?' Molly asked.

'Approximately ten million years,' said Adali.

Michael stood up, faced Adali and thrust his chest forward.

'Do you really expect us to believe that?' he said.

Molly gasped.

'Michael! You're being incredibly rude!' she said. 'What's wrong with you?'

'Nothing's wrong with me!' Michael snapped. Then suddenly, he exploded. 'I'm sick of you keeping secrets from me!' he screamed. His voice was so loud, and of such a high pitch, it hurt Molly's ears. 'You're just like my mum!' he shouted. 'One secret after another!'

Molly stared at her friend, trying to understand what he was saying. As far as she could remember, the only secret she had kept from him was that Adali and Adaline were the same being. And she had only done that because Yosia had told her to. She was about to explain that to Michael when he slumped to the ground, threw his head in his hands, and started sobbing. She looked at Yosia, hoping he might know what to do, but he just sat there, looking at Michael with sadness in his eyes and creases across his brow.

Molly's instinct was to comfort Michael with a hug, but experience had taught her he did not like that. So she just sat there, staring at him, feeling helpless and worried as he continued to sob. Without warning, Adali opened one of her wings and wrapped it around Michael's shoulders. The boy leaned into the wing, as though surrendering to Adali's kindness, and sobbed even more loudly. A moment later, Adali wrapped her wing all the way around Michael's body and lifted him to her chest. Then, like a mother with her newborn baby, she cradled the boy in both her wings and slowly rocked him from side to side.

Molly could hardly believe what she was seeing. She knew that giving comfort during difficult times was the most natural thing in the world, but this was something different. This was healing. Adali was healing Michael from all the distress he had ever felt in his life, not just what he was feeling in this moment. And she was doing it without words.

For the next few moments, Molly listened to the changing volume of Michael's sobs and the burbling of his words. She did not know what he was saying. She only knew he was releasing weeks, months or maybe years of distress. And when Michael finally stopped crying, he just lay there in Adali's arms, still and silent. Molly felt the silence as a stillness in herself and everything around her. Yosia was still, too. He just sat on the edge of the rock, staring into the center of the lake.

Finally, Michael sat up and wiped his face then gazed down at Molly.

'I'm sorry, Molly,' he said. 'I don't know where that came from, but I'm fine now.'

Molly and Yosia both exhaled a sigh of relief. The tension had finally been broken, Molly knew, and the air felt lighter.

'Human emotions build up, like the pressure inside a volcano,' said Adali.

Michael sighed.

'I see that now,' he said. 'Thank you, Adali.'

Adali nodded.

'Are the other six guardians as kind as you?' Michael asked.

'I'm neither kind, nor unkind,' Adali replied. 'I'm simply responding to your energy.'

Molly was bursting with questions. The other guardians - the tree kangaroo, wallaby, tree frog, fruit bat, crocodile, and rainbowfish - do they also change into human form? If so, do they speak with other humans during those hours? Do they keep their double identity a secret from other humans? Do they feel alone, as Adali had once said she did? Do they meet with each other? If so, how often? And do they meet here, in this sacred place? Does each guardian have their own unique magical power? How far would they go to protect the plants and animals? Are there guardians like these in other parts of the world?

She knew it would be impolite to ask these questions while Michael was still recovering, so she kept quiet. But only for a moment.

'Do the other six guardians have the ability to change into human form, too?' she asked.

'Yes,' said Adali. 'Over time, we have evolved to take the form of the most advanced species on Earth. This helps us to do our work as guardians.'

Adali lowered Michael to the ground. For several moments, he stood at her feet, staring into her eyes and nodding. Molly knew Adali was speaking to Michael and no one else. And she saw something in the boy's face she had never seen before. Peace. There was not a single frown, line, or fold on the boy's face. His skin was smooth and clear, almost translucent, and his eyes were sparkling like the ocean on a sunny day.

He sat beside Molly then leaned closer.

'It's okay, Molly,' he said. 'Ask your questions.'

Molly looked up at Adali.

'I have so many questions, I hardly know where to start!' she said. 'Is this place real? Or are we imagining it?'

'This is real,' Adali replied. 'Everything here is real. The stones, lake and sky are all real. They exist in an alternate dimension to the one you occupy, but one that is just as real.'

'Wow,' said Michael. 'Is this the fourth dimension?'

'No,' Adali replied. 'Time is the fourth dimension. We don't have a number for this place. We just refer to it as *our place*.'

'Can we swim in this lake?' Molly asked.

'You can,' said Adali. 'But the sensation will be different to what you're accustomed to.'

'What will it feel like?' Molly asked.

'Find out,' Adali replied.

Molly nudged Michael.

'Are you game?' she asked.

'Sure,' he said.

'I'll join you, too,' said Yosia, standing up.

Molly edged forward and peered down the side of the great, cone-shaped stone. The curve was so steep, she felt certain she would fall straight down to the bottom if she even tried to climb down. So she was shocked when Yosia simply walked down the stone with his body perpendicular to it. Michael burst out laughing.

'No way!' Molly squealed. 'This can't be happening!'

'It is,' said Adali.

Michael went next, and Molly followed him. After only a few steps she felt this way of walking was completely natural. It somehow felt more natural than the awkward posture she would have to bend herself into if she climbed down the face of a steep rock in the real world. Best of all, she could see the entire lake while walking like this.

She was not sure how long it had taken to reach the edge of the lake, because she felt that time was different in this place. On the one hand, it felt as though she might have taken an hour to walk down the stone because it was so enormous, and she was so small. But on the other hand, it had only felt like a few seconds had passed, by the time she had completed her descent.

'Time seems to be slowing *and* speeding,' she said. 'I don't know what to make of it.'

'I know what you mean,' said Michael. 'It's very strange.'

Now standing at the edge of the lake and gazing across its surface, Molly breathed in deeply but there was nothing to smell, and there was no breeze. The lake looked pearlescent, as though it was made from soft pink and blue swirls. Yosia was already standing in it, up to his waist, but Molly was not so confident. She looked at Michael.

'Are you going in?' she asked.

'Yeah,' he said. 'It's just a matter of when.'

'When,' Molly echoed. 'In a place that has such a strange passage of time, the word *when* seems pointless.'

Michael laughed, then stepped into the lake. His feet disappeared as the shimmering shapes enveloped his ankles.

'What does it feel like?' Molly asked.

'Nice, but different from water' he replied. 'Try it.'

Molly took one step into the lake. It did not cover the surface of her skin like water does. Instead, it seemed to sink into her skin.

'It feels more like oil than water,' she said.

'Yeah, it is!' said Michael.

Yosia turned and smiled at them.

'And yet it's not,' he said. 'This lake is every bit as inorganic as the rocks.'

Molly looked up at Adali, seeking confirmation of Yosia's statement. The bird appeared as a tiny speck in the distance, perched atop the great stone, so Molly did not expect Adali would see her face or hear her words.

'It's true,' said Adali.

'My goodness, you sound as though you are right next to me,' said Molly.

'She does,' Michael whispered.

'Um, hang on,' said Molly. 'If this place has no organic life in it, how did it give birth to the seven guardians?'

'Good point!' said Michael.

'That's the great mystery,' Adali replied. 'We have yet to understand it ourselves.'

'Have you discussed it with the other guardians?' Molly asked.

'Many times,' Adali replied.

'Do the others speak as you do?' Michael asked. 'Through their thoughts, I mean.'

'Yes,' said Adali.

'What do you talk about?' Molly asked.

'The natural ecosystem,' Adali replied. 'It is our sole focus.'

Molly liked the idea of speaking about nothing but the natural world. But her joy soon changed to a sinking feeling as she recalled the problem of chemical leaching from the mine, the contaminated lake inside the volcano and the strange experiments on the plants and animals. She knew she had to find a way to stop Symbiotica from damaging the ecosystem. *But how*, she asked herself. How could one girl convince a bunch of adults to change their ways?

Suddenly Molly noticed the surface of the lake was embracing her neck.

'What?' she said. 'Did I wade out this far?'

No one answered her, so she figured she might have only thought the question and forgotten to ask it out loud. She looked up at the top of the stone where Adali appeared as an even tinier speck than before, and she panicked.

'How far have I walked?' she shouted.

'Not far,' Adali replied.

Molly ran back, toward the edge of the lake and somehow arrived in, what felt like, a second. Michael was there waiting for her. She looked around.

'Where's Yosia?' she asked.

'Up there,' Michael replied, pointing to the top of the stone.

'How long was I in the lake for?' Molly asked.

Michael shrugged his shoulders then laughed.

'I don't know,' he replied. 'I no longer have a sense of time.'

'Me neither,' said Molly. 'But I feel it's time to go.'

She walked toward the base of the stone then pressed the sole of her foot against it. A moment later, she was walking up the stone, perpendicular to it, as before.

'I could really get used to this way of walking,' she said.

'It's awesome,' said Michael. 'I feel weightless, but not sick like I did the time I entered a zero-gravity chamber.'

'When was that?' Molly asked.

'Last year,' he replied. 'Mum and Dad took me to the Kennedy Space Center in America. We got to float around inside a Boeing 747 aircraft for a couple of hours.'

'That must have been fun,' said Molly.

'You would think so, but I just spewed the entire time,' Michael replied.

'That's gross.'

When they reached the top of the rock, Molly watched Adali lift Michael onto her foot. The boy ran to her leg and wrapped his arms around it then pressed the side of his face into her soft, gooey skin. Yosia jumped up beside him then offered his hand to Molly. She took it and, with one swift move, he pulled her up. Then she, too, wrapped her arms around Adali's leg and closed her eyes, enjoying the sensation of the bird's soft feathers brushing against her forehead. A moment later, Molly saw the bright white light as Adali secured her and her friends for liftoff.

11

HATCHING A NEW PLAN

Adali landed gently on the ground behind Yosia's hut.

'I guess it's lunchtime,' said Michael.

He rolled down Adali's foot then onto the ground. Then he stood up, brushed the grey dirt from his clothes and smiled at Molly. Yosia jumped down to the ground then lifted Molly down beside him. As her feet hit the ground, Molly knew she was looking forward to some refreshments with her parents.

'I hope you both will join us,' she said, looking up at Yosia and Adali.

'Yes, thanks, Molly,' Yosia replied. 'But first, we need to huddle together so Adali can return us to our usual size.'

For a moment, Molly was not sure what Yosia was talking about. Everything felt normal. But when she looked up at Yosia's bamboo furniture, almost the size of a building in central Sydney, and his hut, which was so enormous, she could not even see the top of it, she remembered.

'Oh, yeah,' she giggled.

She wrapped one arm around Yosia and the other around Michael then the trio closed their eyes. A moment later, Molly became aware of a bright light around her and a sensation of warmth. It felt just as nice as before, and she knew she would never grow tired of the sensation.

'Okay, you can open your eyes,' she heard Yosia say.

When Molly opened her eyes, she saw Michael and Yosia standing beside her. Both were about three quarters the height of Yosia's hut and she, herself, was about half Yosia's height.

'Situation normal,' she said.

Adali chirped from Yosia's shoulder.

'Darling Adali,' said Molly. 'Thank you *so much* for that adventure.'

Adali cocked her head to the side and gazed at Molly, her black eyes twinkling.

'Shall we venture inside?' asked Molly.

'I'm always up for a snack,' Michael replied.

As soon as they stepped into the house, Molly saw her father at the dining table, hunched over the Jeffries' notes.

'Still at it, Dad?' she asked. 'You're missing a beautiful day outside.'

Her father sighed, leaned back in his chair, removed his glasses, and rubbed his eyes.

'I know,' he groaned. 'But I'm determined to get through this.'

'May the four of us enter?' Michael asked.

'Four?' Molly's mother echoed, dumping a set of placemats on the edge of the table.

'Yes,' said Molly. 'Me, Michael, Yosia and Adali. The Fantastic Four.'

'Sure,' her father replied, waving them in. 'Give your mother a hand, though, muppet.'

Molly laid the placemats around the table, then the knives and forks.

'May I help, Mrs. Marsh?' Yosia asked.

'Thanks, Yosia,' her mother replied. 'If you could grab the wok from the stove, and put it on the table, that would be great.'

Molly got out of the way as Yosia carried the enormous wok to the table. As he placed it on the table, she could see it was filled with a riot of noodles and vegetables.

'I must say, your timing is impeccable today,' said Molly's mother.

Molly glanced at Adali, sensing she may have been the architect of this miraculous timing.

'Darling, could you put those papers aside, please?' her mother said.

Molly's father did so then pulled Molly onto his knee and wrapped his arms around her.

'My little muppet,' he said. 'What would I do without you?'

'I dunno,' said Molly.

'My life would be meaningless without you, my little smarty-pants,' he said.

Molly sighed.

'I'm glad you feel that way, Dad, because we have got a lot of things to sort out,' she said.

'Do we now?' her father asked.

Molly glanced a Michael, cradling Adali in one hand and stroking her with one of his other. The bird started cooing which made Yosia smile.

'She's a lovely little thing,' said Molly's mother, sitting down.

Molly cringed at her mother's words. To describe one of the most powerful and magical beings on the planet as *a lovely little thing* seemed absurd. But, of course, her mother did not know the truth about Adali. Very few people did. As far as Molly could tell, it was only her, Michael and Yosia who knew the truth. Perhaps Gideon, too, she imagined.

'What's on your mind?' her father asked.

Molly got off her father's lap and stood beside him.

'Well, we know that Symbiotica has been doing bad things like causing earthquakes and contaminating the water and engineering plants that should not exist,' she said. 'We just need to figure out why they are doing these things and make them stop.'

'We will, muppet,' her father replied.

'Have you discovered anything new in the Jeffries' notes?' Molly asked.

Her father shook his head.

'They've just gone into more detail about the things we already know,' he replied.

'Which is good,' Molly's mother added. 'It will help us to take action.'

Michael looked at Molly's mother.

'Will you share these notes with my mum?' he asked.

'Absolutely!' she replied.

'I'm going to invite your mother to join us here for a chat,' said Molly's father.

Molly was not sure what her father meant by *a chat* and when she glanced a Michael, she noticed him frowning.

'Here's what I'm thinking,' her father continued.

'Tomorrow morning, we should have a breakfast meeting here to discuss the growing body of evidence. I'd like to invite Eddie, too.'

Yosia nodded.

'I will ensure Eddie arrives,' he said.

Michael placed Adali on Yosia's shoulder.

'Can we call my dad, too?' he asked. 'I mean, he's just sitting around in that hospital doing nothing. Surely we can—'

'Yes, absolutely,' said Molly's father. 'I've been thinking about him. Let's call him after lunch.'

As Molly watched everyone filling their bowls with noodles and vegetables, she started to feel better. Finally, a plan was forming. Finally, they were going to take action to protect the plants and animals from the damage that Symbiotica had caused. She just hoped it was not too late. But when her father made the call to Michael's father, her heart sank again because the instant her father mentioned the Jeffries, the call ended.

'What happened?' Michael squealed.

'I don't know,' Molly's father replied. 'Your dad just said he couldn't talk, then he hung up.'

Michael dropped his head in his hands.

Molly's father squeezed the boy's shoulder.

'Don't worry, mate,' he said softly. 'We'll get to the bottom of this. One way or another.'

12

A CHAT WITH ADALINE

As she lay in bed rubbing her swollen belly, Molly knew she had eaten too many roast potatoes at dinner. They had been so yummy, especially with her mother's onion and sage gravy poured all over them. The clock on her bedside table said 11:45 p.m. which meant she and Michael would soon meet with Adaline. As promised, Adali the bird landed on her windowsill and chirped, just to make sure she was awake. She sat up, waved at the bird, then tip-toed down the hallway to get Michael.

When Molly reached the loungeroom, she heard a terrible screeching sound. There was a rhythm to it, so she soon realized it was Michael snoring. She approached toward the couch, which was bulging under the boy's weight, then leaned forward and shook his arm. He flicked her away, but she shook him again.

'Mm?' he said. 'What? Molly? What do you want?'

'Adali has called us to get up,' Molly replied.

'Mm? What?' he muttered.

'Adali has called us to wake so we can meet with Adaline,' Molly repeated. 'Remember?'

'Mm? Yeah. Righto.'

Michael rolled off the couch and landed on the floor with a *thud!*

'Shh!' Molly whispered. 'We can't wake Mum and Dad!'

The boy slowly rose to a standing position.

'Okay,' he whispered. 'Let's go.'

As she descended the back steps, Molly saw Yosia, lurking beside his hut and waving her toward him. She and Michael ran across the grass with no more than the pale moonlight to guide them. But when they followed Yosia to the clearing behind his hut, everything changed.

'Wow!' said Michael. 'It's even more amazing here at nighttime.'

The bamboo chairs were still arranged in a circle around the tiny fireplace. The embers at its center were glowing brightly. Yosia sat down and motioned for Molly and Michael to do the same. Adali hopped off Yosia's shoulder onto her own chair, so Molly knew the transformation was about to begin. She leaned closer to Michael.

'You're about to witness a miracle, my friend,' she whispered.

Michael grunted, keeping his sleepy eyes on Adali.

The bird's feathers ruffled, making her appear twice her usual size. Her neck bent backward and forward several times, then her little beak opened. She let out a strange cry. Molly thought it sounded like a baby crying for its mother, and she wanted to hold the bird just as the bird had held Michael during his moment of need. Instead, Molly kept her hands to herself and watched, as Adali's transformation continued. The bird's wings expanded, about half a meter from each side of her body. She shook them, which caused her feathers to fall to the ground, revealing the prickled brown skin over her delicate bones. Her body widened, then elongated, until her head was higher than the back of the chair. Then she tilted her head back again and let out an awful cry.

'I can't watch,' said Molly, burying her head in her hands.

'I can't *not* watch,' Michael whispered.

When Molly looked up again, she saw an almost human form on the chair. It was slumped forward. A mop of thick, curly, back hair fell over the newly formed legs. The naked brown skin shivered all over, then thickened to form a long brown dress. The woman lifted her head, revealing her strong and slender throat, and breathed in deeply. Then she brought her head to a resting position and gazed at Molly and Michael.

'That was awesome!' Michael shouted.

Adaline looked at him for a moment then turned her attention to Yosia. She stepped toward her husband, placed her hands on his cheeks and kissed him.

'My love,' she whispered.

Yosia placed his hands on Adaline's hips, then pulled her onto his lap. For several seconds, they stared into each other's eyes, making Molly wonder if they had forgotten that she and Michael were still there, watching them.

Finally, Adaline returned her gaze to Molly and Michael then smiled.

'So, my young friends,' she said. 'What are your questions?'

Despite all the questions Molly had been saving for this moment, she was unable to speak. Witnessing this transformation from Adali the bird to Adaline the woman had been just as shocking as when she had witnessed it the other way around several nights previously.

'How does it feel to change like that?' said Michael.

Adaline sighed then shrugged.

'Painful but inevitable,' she replied. 'I have been doing it since the dawn of time.'

'That's ten million years, right?' he asked.

'Yes.'

'So before Yosia came along, who did you hang out with?' Michael asked.

'All souls are eternal,' Adaline replied. 'In a sense, Yosia and I have always known each other.'

Michael grunted then rubbed his eyes.

'It's lovely to see you again, Adaline,' said Molly.

'And you, Molly,' the woman replied. 'I'm aware you have a lot of questions you wanted to ask while I am in human form.'

'Mm,' said Molly, trying to decide where to start. 'Do you and the other guardians have a plan for dealing with Symbiotica and the damage they're causing to the ecosystem?'

Adaline stared into the fire for a moment, before returning her gaze to Molly.

'It is our nature to observe things as they unfold and empower other life forms to take action,' she replied. 'We do not swoop in and fix problems. We are enablers, not heroes.'

Molly saw Michael's shoulders slump. She knew he was disappointed by Adaline's response because he would have preferred a more exciting resolution to the problem. But Molly understood what Adaline was saying.

'An example of that would be helping the network to

grow shields to protect itself from Symbiotica's experiments,' she said.

'Exactly,' said Adaline.

Michael sat up straighter.

'What's the deal with the Ropen?' he asked. 'I mean, it seems to be living in the volcano as one of the many dinosaurs. Is it a dinosaur? '

Adaline frowned.

'Permit me to clarify,' she said. 'The dinosaurs you saw are not the dinosaurs that once roamed the Earth millions of years ago. They are artificial creatures, made by Symbiotica as part of their scientific curiosity. The experiment got out of hand, so Symbiotica shifted those creatures to the volcano where they would not be found.'

'But we found them,' said Molly.

Adaline smiled.

'You found them because you were innocent and unaware of the dangers around the volcano,' she said. 'No one else would have dared venture there. We are all aware of the dangers.'

'By danger, are you referring to the Ropen?' Michael asked.

'Yes,' said Adaline. 'But do not confuse the Ropen with the dinosaurs. They are completely different creatures. The Ropen was born of this Earth at the same time as the guardians.'

'Ten million years ago?' Michael asked.

'Yes,' said Adaline. 'We believe it emerged from the same realm as the guardians.'

'Oh! So, it's one of the guardians!' said Molly. 'That makes perfect sense. After all, it was guarding the volcano, so it —'

'No,' said Adaline. 'It is *not* one of the guardians.'

Molly felt a wave of silence wrap around herself and Michael.

'Let me explain,' said Adaline. 'In your human scientific terms, you talk about DNA, right?'

'Yes,' said Molly and Michael.

'You may have heard the term *junk DNA*,' Adaline continued.

'I'm not sure,' said Molly.

Michael turned toward her.

'The *junk* refers to the parts of our DNA that don't contain any codes or instructions for the cells,' he said. 'It just exists, without serving any useful purpose.'

'So why do we have it?' Molly asked.

Adaline's eyebrows raised and she smiled.

'We believe the so-called junk is potential that is has not yet been realized,' she said. 'But for now, it exists in a dormant state, doing nothing useful.'

Molly could almost feel her brain moving around inside her head.

'So, are you saying the Ropen is the junk DNA of the guardians?' she asked.

'Exactly!' said Adaline. 'The Ropen simply exists without consciousness or awareness. It has an instinct to survive, like all creatures, but it has nothing more.'

'Does it have supernatural powers like the other guardians do?' Molly asked.

'It does,' Adaline said with a shiver. 'But I would prefer not to discuss those in detail.'

'Why?' asked Michael.

'It would not be pleasant for you to hear,' Adaline replied.

Molly leaned back so heavily; she almost knocked the breath out of her body.

Michael smiled at her.

'Aren't you glad you came here, tonight?' he said.

Molly nodded, but she felt a heaviness in her body as she considered how difficult it would be to get past the Ropen to access the dinosaurs inside the volcano.

'We have so much to do, to collect evidence of Symbiotica's work,' she said. 'Then we have to tell people. They deserve to know that strange plants and animals have been created.'

'The time is indeed close, Molly,' said Yosia.

'Did you ever discuss this stuff with the Jeffries?' Molly asked.

Yosia shook his head.

'They kept to themselves,' he replied.

'But my dad obviously knows something about the Jeffries,' said Michael.

'He must do,' Molly agreed. 'He hung up on my dad as soon as he mentioned them.'

Yosia nodded, looking at Michael.

'Your father will be under pressure from Symbiotica to keep quiet about such things,' he said.

'They might even be tapping his phone,' said Michael. 'And Mum's.'

'It's possible,' Molly agreed.

Michael turned toward her.

'It's up to us, Molly,' he said. '*We* have to pull the evidence together and put it in the hands of people who know what to do with it.'

'Agreed,' said Molly, noticing a black leather strap around Michael's neck.

She could not see what was on it because it had fallen inside the boy's t-shirt. For some reason, she needed to know, so she leaned over and tugged it.

'Hey!' said Michael, pushing her hand away.

But Molly was too quick for him. She could see that, dangling from the bottom of the leather strap was the beautiful wooden carving of Adali the bird that Yosia had made for Michael.

'This has been protecting us all along, hasn't it?' she said.

Yosia and Adaline nodded. Then Yosia rested his elbows on his knees and leaned forward.

'There's something I want to tell you both,' he said. 'Adaline, the other guardians and I do *not* want to go to war with Symbiotica. It's not our way.'

'I know,' Molly whispered.

Yosia nodded.

'We believe it's possible that Symbiotica's research may create benefits to our ecosystem in the long run, especially if they can stop traditional mining,' Yosia continued. 'But our concern is the extreme nature of their creations and the fact they are doing that work without speaking to any of the people of this land.'

Molly nodded.

'Which is why we have to quietly gather the evidence and put it in the right hands,' she said.

Michael grunted his agreement.

'Starting tomorrow,' he said. 'When Eddie and my mum meet with us.'

'Yep,' said Molly, yawning.

For several moments, Molly stared into the fire, enjoying the shapes of the flames.

'You should get some sleep, my friends,' said Adaline, smiling.

Molly and Michael stood up, preparing to leave.

Then, to Molly's surprise, Michael said: 'Adaline, may I please give you a hug?'

'Of course!' said Adaline, standing up.

Michael almost leaped over the tiny fireplace to get close to Adaline. He wrapped his arms around the woman's waist, and she held him for what seemed like a long hug. Molly knew this had something to do with the special connection that Michael shared with Adali, but it made her feel sad because she knew Michael wanted to be hugging his mother more than anyone else.

13

BREAKFAST WITH EDDIE

'Yosia, this juice is great,' said Molly.

'Yeah!' said Michael. 'What is it?'

Yosia smiled so wide, Molly could see the red berry stains on his gums.

'It's a combination of papaya, coconut and lemon,' he replied.

Molly's mother shook her head.

'I've tried to make it, but I never get the proportions right,' she said.

Molly put another piece of pancake into her mouth. She let it linger on her tongue for a moment, allowing the banana and honey to melt over her tastebuds. It was *so* good.

'Good morning, everyone,' she heard her father say as he wandered into the kitchen.

Molly noticed his hair was messier than usual and he was frowning at his phone.

'Are you okay, Dad?' she asked.

'Hm?' he said. 'Yes, muppet, I'm fine.'

'You didn't sleep well last night, did you?' said Molly's mother.

Molly's father dropped his phone on the table and stared through the fly screen door. Molly knew he was gazing at the bright blue sky, maybe trying to clear his mind of his concerns.

'Not really,' he replied. 'I listened to too much news before going to bed. The strike at the mine is becoming quite complicated.'

Michael looked down.

'But your mum is a great negotiator,' said Molly's father. 'She'll have this sorted soon.'

'If it helps, Mr. Marsh,' said Yosia. 'I know some of the people involved in organizing the strike.'

Everyone looked at Yosia.

'They're good people,' Yosia continued.

'I'm sure they are,' said Molly's father. 'And I don't blame them for striking. The working conditions down there are worse than I've ever seen. Not to mention the environmental disaster the mine has caused with the drinking water. I just hope we can find a sound solution. And fast.'

Yosia nodded.

'I believe that will be possible,' he said.

Molly had decided there would probably be nothing worse than having dirty water pouring out of the taps in her house. It would mean nothing good to drink, cook with or shower in.

'What's being done to fix the problem?' she asked.

Her father looked at Yosia then at Michael. Molly looked at the boy, too, and she noticed he was still staring at his plate.

'Your plate can't be that interesting,' she said.

Michael sighed then rubbed his forehead.

'I just feel really bad,' he said. 'I mean, it's all our fault!'

'What do you mean, Michael?' asked Molly's mother.

'Us!' said Michael. 'Us Aussies and Americans. We're over here mining the land and making a mess of everything. We shouldn't be here!'

Yosia gave Michael's shoulder a squeeze.

'There's some truth in what you say, Michael, but it's more complex than that,' he said. 'Let's not jump to any conclusions until we've reviewed the evidence with Eddie. And your mother. Is she joining us?'

Michael shrugged, then looked at Molly's father.

'I've sent two text messages to Mrs. Calthorpe, inviting her to this meeting,' he said. 'But I haven't had a response from her, yet.'

Molly was about to start talking about agromining, when she heard someone walking up the back steps of her house. Everyone stared at the back door as a man appeared, wearing the whitest and most freshly pressed shirt Molly had ever seen.

'Wow,' she heard herself say.

'Eddie, man!' said Yosia, standing up. 'It's been a long time.'

'Hey, Yosia!' Eddie replied, opening the door.

Then he glanced at Molly's parents.

'Good morning, Mr. and Mrs. Marsh,' he said, almost bowing.

Molly's father offered his hand.

'It's an honor to finally meet you, Eddie,' he said.

Eddie shook hands with Molly's parents then swiftly turned to Yosia and hugged him. For a moment, Molly saw nothing but a flurry of dark brown hands slapping backs.

Then Eddie looked at Molly and Michael.

'I'm very excited to meet you, Molly and Michael,' he said.

Molly smiled.

'Hello,' said Michael.

'Please sit down, Eddie,' said Molly's mother. 'Can I get you some coffee?'

Eddie's eyes opened wide then he smiled and nodded.

'That would be great,' he replied. 'Thank you, Mrs. Marsh.'

As Eddie settled in, Molly realized she had never met anyone like him before. He seemed so formal, yet so polite and perfect, she wondered if he might be an angel sent from God. Then he looked directly at her and Michael.

'You two are stars,' he said.

Molly and Michael glanced at each other but said nothing.

'I understand you both managed to enter the Symbiotica dome,' he said.

Molly knew Yosia must have mentioned this to Eddie when they had ventured into the volcano to capture a sample from the contaminated lake. That had been almost a week earlier, and she was still curious about the findings of his analysis, but she nodded.

'That was an extraordinary accomplishment,' Eddie continued. 'I can't even find the thing!'

Molly glanced at Michael, suddenly wondering if Eddie was as smart as he seemed.

'Do you think you could show me?' he asked.

Molly's mother shook her head.

'Sorry, Eddie, but we're not planning another break-in,' she said. 'I'm sure you understand the children's safety is our top priority.'

Eddie leaned back.

'Yes, of course, Mrs. Marsh,' he said. 'I'm sorry to be presumptuous. I didn't mean t—'

'No worries, mate,' said Molly's father. 'We have a new piece of the puzzle to share with you.' Then he checked his phone and frowned. 'Philippa still hasn't replied!' he said.

Molly's mother glanced at Michael.

'I'm sure she's still busy,' she said.

Molly's father slid his hands under the table and pulled out a shallow shelf. Upon it was the pile of Jeffries' notes bound with a piece of string. He handed the bundle to Eddie.

'In here, you'll find detailed notes from the Jeffries,' he said. 'They lived in this house before we did, then vanished without a trace, about a month ago.'

Eddie's eyes widened again, but Molly's father continued.

'They've made several comments about bullying in the mine,' he explained. 'It seems that anyone who reported dangerous levels of seismic activity or contamination of the slurry, or the poor containment of the slurry was bullied and threatened. And that's just the beginning of the problems. They've raised other questions about Symbiotica's current and future research plans.'

Eddie eyed the pile of documents.

'The whole thing is getting stinkier by the second,' he said.

Molly's father nodded.

'I have no doubt this is the reason for the Jeffries' sudden disappearance,' he said. 'Which is why I'm passing this problem to you, Eddie. I hope you understand me.'

Eddie nodded.

'Of course, Mr. Marsh,' he said. 'An investigative journalist never reveals the source of their information.'

Molly's mother exhaled and leaned back.

'We understand and respect that,' said Molly's mother. 'But the point Oliver was trying to make is this - we don't want the kids explore to any more risk.'

Eddie gasped then shook his head.

'Absolutely not,' he said. 'I completely understand.'

Molly found this discussion among the adults both strange and interesting. Her curiosity was making it more difficult, by the second, for her to keep quiet. She leaned forward and stared at Eddie.

'Have you completed your analysis of the slurry leach?' she asked.

'Indeed, I have,' Eddie replied.

He glanced at Yosia then at Molly's parents.

'The sample was twenty-seven percent sulfuric acid and seventy-two percent water. The remaining one percent is a complete mystery,' he said.

Everyone stared at him.

'What do you mean it's a mystery?' asked Molly.

'I mean, it's a mystery,' Eddie repeated. 'My testing kit could not identify it. It couldn't even find a broad category for it. I took the sample, along with my analysis, to a friend who works in the biochemistry lab at the university, but she couldn't identify it, either.'

Molly's mind was racing. She felt certain the mysterious chemical must have been the cause of the strange plants and animals she had seen inside the volcano and the dome.

'Surely this mysterious chemical has been invented by Symbiotica,' she said. 'As part of their weird research on the plants and animals, I mean.'

'Animals?' her mother echoed. 'I thought the dome only contained plants.'

Molly felt her heart sink and her face burn as she realized she had just talked herself into a corner. She glanced at Michael. The boy's face was blank, as though he had not yet realized what she had done. His eyes were red, too, so Molly knew he was worrying about his mother.

'True,' said Eddie. 'But Molly and Michael also found animals inside the volcano.'

Molly felt her parents' gaze upon her. All four eyes appeared cold and angry.

'What volcano, Molly?' her father asked.

Molly felt herself shrinking. She wanted to shrink further, so she could crawl into the fold between the seat and the backrest and never see her parents' anger again.

'Answer the question, Molly,' her mother said.

Molly glanced at Michael. This time, the boy's face showed an understanding of the difficult position she had talked herself into. His face flushed, then he cleared his throat and leaned forward.

'Mrs. Marsh, I'd like to explain,' he said.

Molly's mother glared at him.

'Shortly after you all arrived here, Molly and I went for a walk through the plantation,' he explained. 'When we got to the end of the path, we found ourselves at the base of the volcano, so we climbed up for a look, and—'

'What?' Molly's father shouted, standing up. 'The big volcano over there?' he asked, pointing.

Molly knew everyone could see the pale brown volcano in the distance.

'Yes,' said Michael. 'What we found down there wa—'

Molly's father slapped his hand on the table.

'Molly!' he shouted. 'Do you have any idea how dangerous that was?'

'Yes, Dad,' Molly replied. 'I'm sorry. We didn't mean to do anything silly. We just—'

Molly saw Yosia and Eddie exchange glances, both uncomfortable.

Molly's father stared at Yosia.

'Did you know about this?' he shouted.

Yosia nodded.

'Some time after the fact, Mr. Marsh,' he replied.

'How could you keep this from me?' Molly's father shouted.

Molly's mother reached up and took his hand.

'Sit down, darling,' she whispered. 'You can't get cross with Yosia. He's not a babysitter.'

'I am *not* a baby!' Molly shouted.

Molly's father shot a look at her that made her feel as though she might evaporate.

'If you keep doing stupid things, we will have to treat you like a baby!' he shouted.

'That's not fair!' Molly shouted, standing up.

Before she knew it, everyone was shouting. She was not sure how long it went on for. She only knew it ended with Michael standing up and shouting louder than anyone else.

'This is almost as bad as my house!' he shouted, his face wet with tears.

Everyone stared at him.

'Please,' he sobbed. 'Can we just sit down and figure out what to do about my mum? I mean, we still haven't heard from her, have we?'

Molly's father checked his phone again, then gave Michael a sad smile.

'Sorry, mate,' he said.

The Marsh family trio sat down and took a moment to regain their composure. Then all eyes returned to Eddie. He stared back, carefully looking from one person to the next, then sighed.

'We're all in a difficult situation,' he said. 'But there's hope. The chemical analyses from the slurry leach and the lake inside the volcano are a great start. I also have photos of both. And these papers from the Jeffries are an excellent addition. I will pull it all together tonight and compile a briefing note for my Member of Parliament.'

Molly did not know what a *Member of Parliament* was, but she guessed it would be someone important, someone who could stop the damage being done to the plants and animals.

'There's just one more thing I need,' Eddie continued.

He looked at Molly and Michael then at Yosia.

'As far as I can tell, you three are the only people who can find the dome and enter it,' he said.

Molly's mother's eyes looked wild with fear.

'That can't be true,' she said. ' Symbiotica's employees must be able to get in. Heck, Philippa's been inside. She told us that the other day!'

Yosia nodded.

'That's true, Mrs. Marsh,' he said. 'Symbiotica

employees know how to find it, and they enter it by slicing through the wall with laser guns.'

Molly's mother's shoulders slumped.

'That's awful,' she said. 'Nevertheless, the kids are not going back there. They've already been exposed to too much danger.'

Eddie nodded.

'It's okay, Mrs. Marsh,' he said. 'I wasn't going to ask them to enter the place again. Yosia can lead me in. My comment was simply an observation that the kids were able to access the place.'

'It's true,' said Yosia. 'I'm one of a few people who can pass through the wall. For that reason, I was surprised to learn that Molly and Michael had done it, too.'

Molly's father looked at her, then at Michael, his eyes twinkling.

'They're smart and sensitive kids,' he said.

Yosia nodded then looked at Eddie.

'When do you want me to let you in?' he asked.

'Tomorrow morning,' Eddie replied. 'I'll collect you from here at dawn. I'll be accompanied by Sergeant Nalong, a friend with an off-road vehicle.'

Yosia nodded.

'That will certainly be faster than walking,' he said. 'I suggest we invite Gideon to join us.'

'Excellent,' said Eddie.

Molly saw her parents lean back in their chairs and relax. Her father sighed loudly.

'Thanks, guys,' he said. 'We shall leave it in your capable hands.'

14

MRS. CALTHORPE IS MISSING

For several minutes after Yosia and Eddie had left the house, Molly found herself unable to move from her chair. Her arms were folded, and she was sulking. She felt angry with her parents for treating her like a baby. Especially because she and Michael had discovered the plants and animals in the belly of the volcano, and the Symbiotica dome in the jungle. She and Michael had also figured out the connection between the two contaminated lakes and come up with a theory for Symbiotica's reasons for doing their strange research. Agromining. She had known it before her father had even found the Jeffries' notes about it.

Despite her courage and cleverness, her parents were obviously going to make her stay at home while Yosia, Gideon and Eddie got to explore the dome with Sergeant Nalong. It simply was not fair. She stared at Michael, curious about his opinion, but the boy looked too exhausted and upset to care. The dark circles under his eyes seemed to have darkened and the lines on his forehead were getting deeper.

'What's wrong?' she whispered.

Michael frowned at her.

'My mum's missing,' he said. 'Am I the only one who cares?'

Molly's father looked at his phone again.

'Sorry, Michael, she still hasn't replied,' he said.

Michael's eyes watered and his jaw clenched.

'I'm going back to the dome tomorrow with Yosia and Eddie,' he said.

'What?' said Molly's father.

'I need to do something useful,' Michael explained. 'I can't just sit here!'

Molly saw her father's face soften. For a second, she thought he was going to agree to Michael's plan. But his lips pressed together, forming the stubborn white line she knew too well.

'I'm sorry, Michael, but I can't allow that,' he said. 'It's too dang—'

'You can't stop me!' Michael shouted. 'You're not my father!'

Molly felt a surge of excitement as Michael took a stand against her father.

Her father's face softened again.

'Fair point, mate,' he said. 'Let's call your father, hey?'

As he dialed, Molly and Michael stared at him.

'Henry? G'day, mate. How are you?' he said.

'Let me speak with him,' said Michael, reaching for the phone.

'Just a moment, Michael,' said Molly's father.

'Henry, have you heard from Philippa?' he asked.

A moment later, he put the phone on the table and stared at it.

'What's happening *now*?' Michael cried, his eyes welling with tears.

Molly's father sighed.

'I really don't know,' he replied.

'Well? Has he heard from my mum?' Michael asked.

Molly's father stared at his phone again.

'I'm sorry, Michael, but he said *no*,' he replied. 'And then the call ended.'

'I'm sure his phone just lost reception,' said Molly's mother. 'He'll call back.'

The phone rang, and everyone jumped.

'Thanks for calling back, Henry,' said Molly's father. 'Listen, Michael's going to kill me if I don't let him speak with you.'

He handed the phone to Michael.

'Dad? Yeah? Not bad,' said Michael. 'I miss you. Yeah. I know. Can't wait.'

Molly and her parents turned away, giving Michael some privacy.

'I'm really worried about Mum,' Michael cried. 'Na. When was that? So, what's going on?'

Michael dropped his head into his hand. He was quiet for a moment then he returned the phone to Molly's father.

'Dad would like to speak to you in private,' he said.

As Molly's father took the phone into the lounge-room, Molly felt certain he was receiving bad news. Michael might have thought so, too, because he started to cry. Molly's mother wrapped her arm around him.

'It's okay, Michael,' she whispered. 'There will be a sensible explanation for this.'

But Molly could tell her mother was just as worried as Michael was. Molly strained her ears to hear her father's conversation with Mr. Calthorpe. Her father was not doing much speaking, and when he did speak, it was just to say: 'aha' or 'okay' or 'ah, geez'. It seemed to last forever, so when he finally returned to the dining table, Molly wanted to shake the news out of him.

'Please tell me what's going on,' said Michael.

Molly's father sighed and sat down. Then he looked at Michael.

'Your dad says he hasn't spoken to your mum for several days,' he said. 'But don't despair, Michael. If you remember, we saw your mum here yesterday afternoon.'

'No, Dad, that was the day before,' said Molly. 'It's been almost forty-eight hours since we've seen Mrs. Calthorpe.'

Molly's father stared at the table.

'Let's just sit tight,' he said. 'There will be a perfectly reasonable explanation.'

But Molly was not so sure. And she could feel Michael's despair circling the room, pressing down on everyone. More than anything, she wanted to tell Michael there was no need to worry, but she could not because she was just as worried.

'I have an idea!' she said.

Michael looked up, his eyes red.

'What?' he asked.

'Tomorrow morning, when Sergeant Nalong comes to collect Yosia and Gideon, we will tell him about your mum,' she said. 'After all, Sergeant Nalong is a policeman, right?'

Michael shook his head.

'I don't want to wait until then,' he said. 'Forty-eight hours is long enough. Please, Mr. Marsh, just call the police now.'

Molly's father glanced at her mother. She nodded.

'I think that's appropriate, darling,' she said.

Molly's father nodded, then tapped the emergency number on his phone.

'Put it on speaker, Dad,' said Molly.

Everyone crowded around the phone and stared at it.

'Police Operations,' said the voice.

'I need to report a missing person,' said Molly's father.

Molly, her mother, and Michael all nodded as Mr. Marsh provided a physical description of Mrs. Calthorpe. Every detail - from her wild mop of frizzy grey hair to her height and weight and the clothes she was wearing when she had visited them two days prior - and he was just as precise as Molly expected from her father.

'Thank you,' said the operator. 'Please tell me where and when you last saw her.'

'Exactly forty-eight hours ago,' said Molly's father. 'Here at my house.'

Then Molly's father provided his name and address.

'What was the last thing she said to you?' the operator asked.

'She just said she had to go. I didn't ask her where she was going because she was under enough pressure as it was. She's the Chief Operating Officer at the copper mine, and—'

'But the mine is closed now,' said the operator.

'It's closed temporarily, but Philippa's work doesn't stop,' Molly's father explained. 'In fact, it's become much worse because she's under pressure from her boss in Australia, and the bigger boss in America. Not to mention the media and activist groups here. We know she's extremely busy, but we're worried because she hasn't responded to a single message.'

'Thank you, Mr. Marsh,' said the operator. 'I've captured all these details and will relay them to all of our police cars and units, now. If we get any leads, we'll let you know.'

'What?' said Molly's father. 'Is that it? Surely you can take more active measures to—'

'I'm sorry, Mr. Marsh,' said the operator. 'We're under pressure here, too, with the civil unrest over the mining activity and the contaminated water supply. But I assure you, we'll do our best, and we'll get back to you as soon as we have something to tell you. Goodbye.'

'Argh!' Michael screamed, slapping his hand onto the surface of the table.

No one rushed to offer him words of comfort because no one knew what to say any more. But Molly had an idea.

15

LET'S ASK ADALI

By the time Molly got Michael into the back garden, Eddie had left and Yosia was there alone, raking the fallen leaves into neat piles. Adali was perched on his shoulder. When she saw Molly and Michael approach, she chirped in Yosia's ear, and he turned toward them.

'Hello, you two,' he said.

'Yosia, we have a big problem,' said Michael.

Yosia dropped his rake and stared at the boy. Adali cocked her head to the side and cooed. Then, without a word of introduction, Michael launched into the problem. He repeated the entire telephone conversation Molly's father had just had with the Police Operator.

'How can they expect us to just sit here and wait!' he shouted. 'What if they never find her?'

Adali jumped up and down on Yosia's shoulder, squawking. Yosia nodded at her then looked at Michael.

'Okay, here's the plan,' he said.

Adali took to the air and flew away.

'Where's she going?' Michael shrieked.

'She's going to enter your house and look around,'

Yosia replied. 'If there's no evidence of your mother having been there in the last twenty-four hours—'

'How would Adali know that?' Michael asked.

Molly cleared her throat then nudged Michael.

'She's Adali,' she said. 'She knows everything.'

Michael nodded then shoved his hands into his pockets.

'As I was saying,' Yosia continued. 'If Adali doesn't see any evidence of your mother's recent presence in the house, she will enter the mine and—'

'Let me go with her!' said Michael. 'I know the mine. I've been there!'

'Adali knows the mine, too,' Yosia said. 'She's lived here a long time, Michael.'

'Sure. Sorry,' said Michael.

'If Adali can't find your mother in the mine, she'll check the dome,' Yosia continued.

Michael's shoulders dropped, and his breathing slowed.

Yosia placed his hand on the boy's shoulder.

'In the meantime, Michael, please don't panic,' he said. 'There will be a sensible explanation. For all we know, she might have lost her phone somewhere along the way.'

Molly had not considered that possibility.

'That's a good point,' she said. 'Once, my dad's phone ran out of battery power when he was out, and mum panicked because she couldn't get through to him, but he was fine.'

'Yeah, okay,' said Michael. 'We'll sit and wait, then.'

'Oh, look, there she goes,' said Molly, pointing at the Calthorpe's kitchen window.

The bird flew out of the window, then darted down the street.

'Okay, she's heading for the mine,' said Yosia. 'She might be gone for a while, but don't panic. She's very thorough. Trust me, she will inspect every detail in the place!'

Molly gripped Michael's forearm and brought him over to the picnic blanket.

'Sit down,' she said.

Michael flopped onto the ground with his shoulders slumped forward and his belly protruding so much, Molly imagined he could fit a whole cow in there. Then she felt a strange sensation in her own belly. It was the sinking feeling she often got when she knew things might not work out the way she had hoped. Deep in her bones she knew the police were too busy to look for Mrs. Calthorpe. It would be up to Michael and her to do that.

'I have an idea,' she said.

Michael sighed.

'What?'

Molly paused for a moment, thinking about the best way to say what was on her mind.

'If your mum is not found by tomorrow morning, we should look for her in the dome,' she said.

Yosia approached.

'That's not going to happen, Molly,' he said.

'Why not?'

'Firstly, Adali is already searching for Mrs. Calthorpe, as you know,' he replied. 'Furthermore, your parents have been explicit in their wishes that you stay at home.'

Molly knew Yosia was correct on both points, but

she was determined to get back inside the dome. She wanted to help collect the evidence. And, for reasons she could not explain, she felt certain Mrs. Calthorpe was there.

16

A SILENT SUPPER

Molly, her parents, and Michael passed the bowls of food around the table without saying a word. It was as though everyone knew it would be pointless to even try to make conversation. Each person was lost in their own swamp of worry about the situation, Molly knew. To make matters worse, the police had not called and Adali had not returned, despite leaving Yosia's shoulder more than six hours earlier.

Yosia appeared at the back door.

'Yosia! Please join us!' said Molly's mother, with even more enthusiasm than usual.

Molly suspected her mother was desperate for an extra person at the table. Anything to lift the tone of the evening. But Yosia looked just as unhappy as everyone else.

'It's okay. I'll come back when you've finished your dinner,' he said.

'No, mate. Seriously. Please join us,' said Molly's father.

As Yosia stepped inside, Molly could see his face was longer and thinner than usual.

'Are you okay?' she asked.

Molly's mother looked concerned, too.

'Please, Yosia, sit down,' she said.

She fetched another dinner plate from the kitchen cupboard then brought it to the table and filled it with the vegetable curry and rice. It was one of Molly's favorite dishes. The combination of carrots and raisins made her tastebuds sing so she was pleased she still had half of it left on her plate.

'Please don't go to any trouble, Mrs. Marsh,' said Yosia.

'It's no trouble at all,' Molly's mother insisted.

Molly had several questions for Yosia, but she knew she had to phrase them carefully. She could not say anything that suggested Adali had been talking to Yosia. Her parents would never believe it and they might even decide to keep her at home for more than a day or two.

'Has Adali returned from her flight?' she asked.

Yosia shook his head.

Molly's parents frowned at her.

'Are you referring to Yosia's pet bird?' Molly's mother asked.

Molly almost choked on a mouthful of rice. Having witnessed the supreme magical gifts of Adali and Adaline, she felt uncomfortable about someone referring to her as a *pet*. She was glad to see Yosia was not offended, even though she knew he was too worried to feel anything else. And Michael was worried about his mother.

Molly knew she would have to be strong for them

both, but it was difficult because her mind was spinning through the limited facts, each time coming up with more questions. All she knew was that Mrs. Calthorpe had been missing for over two days and Adali had been gone for six hours. Had Adali found Mrs. Calthorpe? If so, was she helping the woman to get back home? Were they in danger? If so, what kind of danger? Did they need help?

Michael dropped his knife and fork onto his plate, shattering the silence. Then he stared at Molly's father.

'With respect, Mr. Marsh,' he said. 'I'm going into the mine tomorrow morning. My mum *must* be in there, and I need to know she's okay.'

Molly's father looked at Michael for a moment before responding.

'Okay, mate,' he said. 'If you still feel that way tomorrow, I'll join you.'

Molly's mother dropped her cutlery onto her plate, making another unpleasant sound.

'No!' she said. 'How many times have we been through this? It's too dangerous! No one is going anywhere and that's final!'

Molly felt her gut churn with frustration.

'That's not fair, Mum,' she said. 'You can't expect us to just sit here and—'

'Don't you start, Molly,' her mother warned, holding up her finger.

Yosia cleared his throat.

'With respect to everyone,' he said. 'We will *all* make better decisions tomorrow after a good night of sleep.'

Everyone nodded.

'Please excuse me,' he said, standing up.

As Molly watched Yosia leave the house, she felt a pain in her chest. She knew Yosia and Adali had never spent more than a few hours apart and it had been seven hours since the bird's departure.

17

SERGEANT NALONG

The sun had barely risen when Molly joined Yosia in her front garden. The street was completely silent and motionless. Not even the birds were chirping.

'Good morning, Yosia,' she said.

'I'm surprised you're up so early,' said Yosia.

'I just felt like it,' Molly said, stretching.

'No, you didn't,' Yosia argued. 'You just want to hitch a ride to the dome.'

Molly laughed.

'Ah. You got me,' she said.

She sat down beside Yosia, then saw Adali perched on his knee.

'Oh, my goodness, Adali's back!' she said.

Adali chirped a little greeting.

'We were *so* worried about you,' said Molly, stroking the bird's head.

Adali's feathers fluffed up and she cooed.

'Did you find Mrs. Calthorpe?' Molly asked.

'No,' Yosia replied.

'So, what *did* you find?' Molly asked.

Yosia's frown deepened.

'She encountered something troubling inside the dome,' he replied.

'What, exactly?' Molly asked.

Yosia stroked Adali's feathers until they flattened. Then he sighed.

'She found evidence of more hideous research projects in the pipeline,' he replied.

'Like what?' Molly asked.

Yosia gave Molly a sad smile.

'Like engineering more species of plants to absorb the copper from the ground,' he replied. 'Just as you said, Molly, they are agromining. And more.'

'More what?' Molly asked.

'More genetic engineering,' Yosia replied. 'For every strange plant they create, they're planning to engineer three or four new species of animal.'

Molly felt a mild tremor move through her body. She felt cold and sweaty.

Yosia sighed again.

'It's terrifying to think of what might happen to our ecosystem when they release more artificially-created plants and animals.'

Molly felt frightened, too. Another glance at Adali told her the bird was still distressed.

'I presume you're going to inform Eddie and his police friend,' she said. 'And Gideon.'

'I can't,' Yosia replied.

'Why not?'

'I'd have to reveal the source of my information,' Yosia replied, bringing Adali to his chest. 'All I can do is enter the dome and run straight over to the spot where Adali found the evidence. If it's still there, I'll grab it and give it to Eddie. In the meantime, Molly, please keep this information to yourself.'

'I promise,' Molly whispered. 'Can we tell Michael though?'

'Sure,' said Yosia.

Molly rested her head on Yosia's shoulder and closed her eyes.

'Good morning!' she heard a cheery voice behind her.

Yosia turned around.

'Hey, Giddy man,' he said.

Molly was surprised to see that Gideon was wearing shoes and a shirt. Last time she had met him, he was barefoot, scruffy, and only wearing a pair of short pants. But today, he seemed to be ready for action. He approached Yosia, slapped him on the back then sat beside him.

'Hey, Molly,' he said.

'Hi, Gideon,' Molly replied.

She heard more footsteps pounding the ground behind her. As she turned to look, she was expecting to see her father, keen as always to keep an eye on her. But it was Michael. His hair was all over the place and there was a long, deep fold down the side of his face. Molly laughed.

'Morning,' said Michael, straightening his t-shirt.

'Good morning,' Molly replied. 'You're up early.'

'Mm,' Michael grunted, sitting beside her.

Molly was about to ask Michael if he had slept well when she realized she had better use the time to tell Michael what Yosia had just told her.

'Adali found some interesting evidence in the dome,' she said.

Michael nodded.

'I wonder if anyone has seen or heard from my mum,' he said.

Yosia looked at him and shook his head.

'I'm sorry, Michael, but she did not find any evidence of your mother being there,' he replied.

As Michael's shoulders slumped again, Molly heard her mother's voice. But when she looked behind her, she saw both her parents. They were showered, dressed, and holding their coffee cups.

'Good morning, Mum and Dad,' she said. 'This is a nice surprise.'

'Morning, honey,' her mother replied. 'We didn't sleep very well.'

'Wow!' said Michael, pointing to the end of the street.

Everyone looked up as the off-road police vehicle cruised toward them.

'It's enormous!' Molly laughed.

Aside from the bizarre trucks inside the mine, she had never seen a car with wheels as large as the ones on this vehicle. She figured they would have been the same height as her. And from a quick glance of the three rows of seats in the thing, she could tell it would fit at least nine people.

'We might need a ladder to climb inside,' she laughed.

Molly felt her mother's hands gently squeeze her shoulders. It was a warning, she knew, but when Eddie leapt out of the vehicle and waved at them, her mother let go. The man was just as immaculate as he had been the previous day. His white shirt was pressed to crispy perfection and so were his brown pants. Molly had never seen anyone dress this sharp and she wondered if he was expecting a visit from the Queen.

'Good morning, Mr. and Mrs. Marsh,' he said, nodding.

'G'day, Eddie,' said Molly's father. 'How are you, mate?'

'Very well, thank you,' Eddie replied. 'May I introduce—'

The driver of the vehicle approached. He was wearing a khaki shirt and pants. The speckled type with blotches of green and brown. Molly thought they looked more like pyjamas than a uniform.

'Sergeant Nalong,' said Eddie.

Sergeant Nalong extended his hand to Molly's mother.

'Mrs. Marsh,' he said. 'And Mr. Marsh. It's good to meet you both.'

Molly's parents shook his hand.

'And you, Yosia and Gideon,' said the sergeant, shaking hands.

'I suspect we have a big day ahead,' said Yosia.

Sergeant Nalong shrugged.

'I'm not sure we'll find anything,' he said. 'These big companies are very good at covering their tracks. But we should check the place, nevertheless.'

'It's none of my business,' said Molly's father. 'But do you have a search warrant?'

'I do,' the sergeant replied. 'Not that it matters, because it's our land. Furthermore, our intelligence tells us there are rarely any staff in the dome, so I'm not expecting confrontation with anyone. We'll be in and out in less than ten minutes, I'm sure.'

Molly felt like laughing at Sergeant Nalong. The man had no idea what he was talking about. The mysteries in the place, the research documents Yosia had just told her about and the —

'How will you deal with the alarm system?' she asked.

Everyone stared at her.

'You must be Molly,' said Sergeant Nalong. 'And you must be Michael,' he added, nodding at the boy. 'Eddie has told me about you two. You seem to have a knack for getting into the place.'

'Molly also has a knack for setting off the alarm system,' said Michael.

Sergeant Nalong laughed.

'Never mind,' he said. 'We'll avoid doing that.'

'So, is it just going to be the four of you?' Molly asked.

'Yes,' said the sergeant. 'And we should get going.'

He learned forward slightly, almost bowing to Molly's parents.

'Can we go with you?' Molly asked.

Sergeant Nalong's face lit up, as though he thought it was a great idea, but Molly's mother was quick to step in.

'No, honey,' she said, clutching Molly's shoulders. 'We've discussed this already.'

The sergeant paused for a moment, as though thinking about what he wanted to say.

'With respect, Mrs. and Mr. Marsh,' he said. 'There's nothing dangerous about this mission. It will be an easy fact-finding exercise. Nothing more. I feel the kids would be a great asset and — '

'Well, they're *our* kids,' Molly's mother interrupted. 'And we've said no.'

Sergeant Nalong stepped back and bowed again.

'Of course, Mrs. Marsh,' he said. 'Please forgive me.'

He glanced at Yosia, Gideon and Eddie.

'Ready?' he asked.

Yosia nodded, holding Adali against his chest again. As he stepped toward the vehicle, Molly felt her heart sink. She desperately wanted to join them. Michael did, too. She could tell because his shoulders slumped even further, and he let out a load groan.

'Sergeant?' said Molly's father. 'May I see your I.D.?'

'Certainly,' said Sergeant Nalong, retrieving a plastic card from inside his shirt.

Molly watched her father's face as his eyes roamed across the plastic card.

'Military Police,' he said. 'Why would your specialist services be required if, as you say, there will be no confrontation or trouble at the dome?'

Molly's mother huffed.

'Just let the man go,' she said.

But Sergeant Nalong smiled and shrugged his shoulders.

'It's just the luck of the draw,' he replied, returning his card to his pocket. 'Police resources are thinly spread with all the civil unrest. I must have drawn the short straw, so to speak.'

Molly's mother nodded.

'Good luck, then,' she said, waving the sergeant away.

Molly's father made a sound, as though he was going speak. But he was interrupted by Molly's mother.

'Mind your own business, darling,' she muttered.

'It *is* our business if the kids are going with him,' he replied.

'No, they are not!' Molly's mother shouted.

Michael stood up straighter.

'Thanks, Mr. Marsh,' he replied. 'We'll be fine.'

'I know you will,' said Molly's father. 'Because I'm coming with you. After all these wild stories you kids have told me, I want to see this place for myself.'

Molly's mother crossed her arms and shook her head.

Sergeant Nalong stepped a bit closer to her.

'You're very welcome, Mr. Marsh,' he said. 'We have plenty of room. And the more hands we have, to collect the evidence, the better off we'll be. Mrs. Marsh, you are also welcome to join us.'

Molly's mother shook her head.

'No, thank you,' she said. 'I'd like to be here in case Philippa returns.'

'Thanks, Mrs. Marsh,' said Michael.

Molly's mother gave him a smile.

'Would you at least let me cook you all breakfast before you go?' she asked.

Sergeant Nalong shook his head.

'No, thank you, Mrs. Marsh,' he replied. 'We must get going. Besides, we have two big boxes of food and water in the back of the vehicle.'

Molly's mother nodded.

'Fine,' she said.

She placed her hands on Michael's face and stared into his eyes.

'You be careful, young man,' she said. 'But don't get yourself too worried about things, okay?'

'Thanks, Mrs. Marsh,' Michael replied, politely wriggling free of her grip.

She leaned toward Molly and pressed her forehead against Molly's.

'Do not leave your father's side for a moment,' she said.

'I won't, Mum,' said Molly. 'I promise.'

A moment later, Molly felt Michael's hands on her waist, lifting her into the massive vehicle.

'This is awesome!' she said, slapping the seat on either side of herself.

She was pleased to be in the center of the back seat because it gave her a great view of everything around her.

'We're in for a spectacular view,' she squealed, clenching her fists.

But when her father sat on her other side, she suddenly felt squashed between him and Michael because they were both twice her size. She knew they would provide good padding if the vehicle crashed, but she felt closed in.

'Dad, please, could you move?' she asked, pointing to the bench seat opposite.

'What?' he said. 'You don't want your old man sitting next to you?'

Molly knew he was only pretending to be offended. She could also tell he was getting excited about the journey, and she liked that. It was so rare to see him excited because he was always so careful and serious about everything.

'I love you, Dad,' she said. 'But I would also like to have a view.'

Her father shifted to the bench seat opposite, placing himself back-to-back with Sergeant Nalong in the driver's seat. Eddie sat in the front seat beside the sergeant then turned around and smiled. Molly felt certain his bright white teeth would glow in the dark. Even more than his crisp white shirt.

'Seatbelts, everyone!' Eddie sang out as Sergeant Nalong started the engine.

As Yosia sat beside Molly's father, Adali hopped down to his knee.

'Where's Gideon?' Molly asked.

'There,' said Yosia pointing at the back of the vehicle.

'In the boot?' said Molly, turning around.

'It's not a boot,' Gideon called out. 'It's another back seat.'

Sure enough, when Molly stretched over the back of her seat, she saw another back seat and Gideon was sprawled across it.

'Wow,' she laughed. 'Good call, Gideon.'

The vehicle reversed down the driveway. Molly leaned forward to wave goodbye to her mother who was still standing there with her arms folded and her lips pressed together.

'I hope she forgives us, Dad,' said Molly.

'Who? Mum?' her father replied. 'Of course she will!'

But Molly was not so sure about that.

18

BACK TO THE SINKHOLE

As the vehicle descended the steep mountain, everyone gripped their seatbelts. Except for Adali, who hovered in the air, her wings beating louder than the roar of the engine. Molly gripped her stomach, feeling her breakfast of cheesy bread rolls and fruit juice sloshing around. Michael did the same. Then he farted. Loudly.

'Sorry!' he said, his face flushing.

'Oh, dear God,' said Molly's father, winding down the window.

Yosia rolled down another window. Molly laughed but when the stench reached her face, she was quick to move to the nearest window and shove her head outside. Adali did the same. A moment later, Gideon started coughing.

'I don't have a window back here!' he said.

Everyone laughed at him, and the ruckus got Eddie's attention.

'Sorry about the bumps!' he shouted. 'But don't worry, the vehic—What's that smell?'

As the vehicle wound around the side of the mountain, Molly could see the bright green valley. The color was just as she remembered, and the little dots of pink, purple, yellow and white across the surface reminded her of sprinkles on a cupcake.

'Look!' she squealed, nudging Michael's arm. 'You can see the wildflowers from here!'

But Michael did not look excited. His face was set in concentration and discomfort as he clung to his seatbelt with one hand and his belly with the other. Molly decided to keep her distance, just in case the boy's intestines erupted again. The beautiful view, fresh air and morning sunlight were enough to occupy her, and she soon heard the waterfalls thundering the mountain.

'Wow!' her father shouted, pointing at them. 'The bottom of that sinkhole must be drenched!'

'It is, Dad,' said Molly. 'You will love it!'

Suddenly, she felt the same urge she had felt the first time she had visited this place - to stand under the waterfall. She knew it was not yet warm enough to do that, but she felt excited about being inside the sinkhole again.

'Have you been here before, Eddie?' she shouted.

'No!' Eddie shouted back.

'What about you, Sergeant?' Molly asked.

'Once!' the sergeant shouted. 'But I've never been to the bottom, nor have I seen the dome.'

'It's only a hundred meters down,' said Michael.

Molly saw her father frowning.

'What's up, Dad?' she asked.

'There's nothing but water and rocks down there,' he said.

'The dome *is* there, Dad,' Molly insisted. 'It's just invisible.'

Her father frowned, then shook his head, as though

he did not believe her, which made her angry because she had already told him about the invisible dome. And Yosia, Michael and Mrs. Calthorpe had confirmed its existence.

'Mr. Marsh, it's really there,' said Michael. 'It's just cloaked.'

'Cloaked?' Molly's father echoed. 'You said that the other day, mate. What do you mean?'

Michael's face twisted into a pained expression, as though he was explaining high school physics to a kid in kindergarten.

'Like in Star Trek,' he said. 'They use cloaking technology to hide their spaceships from their enemies.'

Molly's father frowned.

'And you believe that's real, do you, mate?' he laughed.

'Don't be rude, Dad,' said Molly. 'Michael's right. You'll see!'

'Okay, you pair of smarties,' said Molly's father. 'How does cloaking technology work? Hm?'

'It's got something to do with the manipulation of light,' Michael replied. 'It's only theoretical, which is why we've never seen it before. Not until now, anyway.'

Molly glanced at Yosia, aware that Adali's main magical powers include the manipulation of light and energy fields. And that thought directed her curiosity to the other six guardians Adali had told her about. What are their magical powers, she wondered. Other than their ability to change into human form for a few hours each day, she knew nothing about them. There had been no time to ask.

But for now, she was excited by the view. The vehicle was reaching the bottom of the mountain, getting closer to the bright green valley. Surrounded by the dark, jungle-covered mountains, it looked like something from a fairytale. Molly thought about the last time she and Michael had been there, trekking across the valley in the midday heat, exhausted and dehydrated. But not this time. This time, she was with her father, and she was going to prove to him that everything she had been saying was true. She felt proud of herself, and she hoped he would be proud of her, too.

Sergeant Nalong stopped the vehicle and switched off the motor. For a moment, the only sound was the waterfalls thundering down the mountains. Everyone stared at them.

'So, this is the famous sinkhole,' said Molly's father.

Molly figured they were about two hundred meters away from the edge of the hole. She was looking forward to the walk, so she opened the door and jumped out. Her father followed, then Sergeant Nalong slipped out, too. A moment later, Eddie was by the sergeant's side. Molly noticed how close they stood, like old souls who had been together forever. She watched Eddie lift a small backpack onto his shoulders while the sergeant removed the coiled rope from his shoulder.

'You won't need that, Sergeant,' said Molly.

The man looked at her; his eyebrows raised.

'It's a long way down, Molly,' he said.

'True,' said Molly. 'But we know a shortcut.'

Sergeant Nalong and Eddie looked at Yosia.

'Molly's right,' said Yosia. 'Let her lead us down.'

Molly felt a surge of power race through her legs as she bounced forward, ready to take the lead. Her father was quick to follow and was soon holding the back of her t-shirt.

'Just remember the promise you made to Mum,' he whispered.

Molly remembered she had promised to stay close to her father. But now she wanted some distance from him because she knew what she was doing, and she was leading this mission.

'It's okay, Dad,' she said.

The sun was low and shining in her eyes as she marched across the vibrant green valley. But squinting was a small price to pay for the adventure, and she knew it would be shady inside the sinkhole. The closer they got to the edge of the hole, the louder the waterfalls became, so Molly did not hear Adali flying overhead. She only saw the dark shape moving through the air and it gave her a fright.

'It's okay!' Yosia called out.

Within seconds, Adali had dive-bombed down the hole.

'She's probably inside the dome by now,' Molly whispered.

'I'd say so,' said Michael.

When they reached the edge of the sinkhole, they all stopped and looked down. As far as Molly could tell, the place looked the same. The internal wall of the hole, shaped like a cylinder, was made from rocks of many shapes and colors. Trees, shrubs, and flowers burst forth from the cracks between the rocks. And the pool of white water at the bottom, churned by the endless pounding of the waterfalls, was surrounded by mud.

Sergeant Nalong sighed.

'It's hard to imagine we have a shortage of drinking water in the town center,' he said.

'Mm,' said Eddie. 'Perhaps this crisis will force the

government to invest in some much-needed engineering to deliver this clean water to the people.'

'That would be nice,' said Yosia.

'So, where's this dome?' Molly's father asked.

Molly groaned.

'It's down there, Dad,' she said. 'You just can't see it yet!'

She looked at Sergeant Nalong.

'May I lead us down, now?' she asked.

'Sure, Molly,' he said. 'After you.'

Molly stepped down to the first large slab of dark grey granite. Protruding over the bottom of the sinkhole, it offered a view she found just as exciting and terrifying as the last time she had stood upon it. But her moment of wonder was interrupted by her father clinging to the back of her t-shirt again. She wriggled free then took another step forward, only to feel him do it a third time.

'Dad, please relax,' she hissed.

'Not for a second, muppet,' he replied.

'But we're going to have an accident if you keep doing that!' Molly insisted.

Her father's only reply was to wrap his arm around her shoulders and pull her closer.

'I won't fall,' Molly insisted. 'I know what I'm doing!'

Aware of Michael, Yosia, Gideon, Eddie, and Sergeant Nalong behind them, Molly was starting to feel closed in. She wanted space to feel her way down to the bottom as she had done the last time. She took another few steps forward then jumped down to the next stone staircase.

'Surely we need to get to that set of steps that goes all the way down,' her father said.

'Yes, Dad, we do,' Molly replied.

She looked at the space between where she stood now and where she needed to go. It was several meters, but she knew how to close the gap. She had done it before.

'Oooip!' she sang.

The stone she was standing upon slowly pivoted to the right, bringing Molly and her father with it.

'Oh, dear God!' he cried, clinging to her.

'It's okay, Dad,' she said. 'It's supposed to do that.'

A moment later, it joined the first in the set of steps that lead to the bottom of the sinkhole. Molly and her father jumped down to the first step.

'That's incredible,' he said, holding her tight. 'But what about the others?'

Molly looked at Michael.

'Call the staircase back toward you!' she shouted.

'Oooip!' Michael sang, sounding as flat as a pancake.

Nothing happened.

'Someone else try!' Molly shouted.

'Oooip!' Yosia, Gideon, Eddie, and Sergeant Nalong shouted.

To Molly's ears, they all sounded off-key; like an orchestra of untuned amateurs.

'I guess it's up to me,' she said.

'Oooip!' she sang.

The massive stone pivoted back toward Michael and the others.

'Are you the only person who can do that?' asked Molly's father.

'I don't know,' Molly replied. 'Maybe.'

'Yes, she is!' Yosia called out, stepping onto the staircase behind Michael.

Gideon stood behind Yosia.

'All aboard!' he shouted.

'Oooip!' Molly sang again.

As the staircase pivoted again, Gideon grabbed Yosia's arm.

'You won't fall, Giddy man,' Yosia laughed.

'Why are you the only person who can activate that stone?' asked Molly's father.

Molly shrugged her shoulders.

'It's one of the many mysteries of the place,' Yosia explained. 'The elements here respond to the energy of people as they move through the space. They seem to like Molly very much.'

Yosia, Gideon and Michael jumped down to the first step beside Molly and her father.

'Yosia, how do you usually get down here?' Molly asked.

'The long way,' he replied. 'The way I took you out of this place last time.'

Molly remembered that walk. They had squeezed into a narrow opening between the rocks at the base of the sinkhole, then hiked up through a long narrow cave inside the mountain. It had been a tough climb. There had been nothing pleasant about it.

'Oooip!' she sang.

The stone pivoted back toward Eddie and Sergeant Nalong. They stepped onto it and clung to each other.

'Oooip!' Molly sang again.

'This really is the strangest thing I've ever seen,' said Molly's father.

'You'll soon see something stranger, Dad,' Molly laughed.

As she descended the steps to the bottom of the sinkhole, Molly was aware of the procession behind her. Her father was directly behind her, still too close for her liking. Behind him were Michael, Yosia, Gideon, Eddie, and Sergeant Nalong. As they got closer to the bottom, Molly started to worry. Would she be able to lead everyone through the invisible wall, she wondered. If so, would Adali be there to greet her? Would there be anyone else inside the dome?

When Molly finally reached the bottom, she noticed the cooling effect of the wet mud on her feet. It felt so nice, she wanted to wade through it and play under the waterfall. But there was serious work to be done, so she turned to face the others.

Michael and Yosia, she noticed, appeared to be relaxed. But her father, Gideon, Eddie, and Sergeant Nalong, all strangers to this place, were fidgeting and glancing around nervously. She was not sure what to say to make them feel better.

'Are you ready to go in?' she asked.

They nodded and smiled, except for her father.

'Dad, I'll go through the wall with Michael, first,' said Molly.

All the color drained from her father's face.

'I'll be okay, Dad. I promise,' she said. 'And I'll be back before you know it!'

Her father's eyes watered then he swallowed hard.

'It will be fine, Mr. Marsh,' said Yosia. 'Molly knows how to handle the elements here.'

Molly motioned to Michael. He stepped behind her and rested his hands on her shoulders. She rested her heels on his toes then lifted her arms.

'I'm ready,' she whispered.

As Michael stepped forward, Molly stretched her

arms as far forward as she could then wriggled her fingers. Soon, she touched the soft gel.

'Hello, again,' she whispered.

A moment later, she felt herself being pulled into the wall as her father's cry of dismay faded in the distance. Soon she was inside the gel matrix, and she could see the soft white glow that told her Adali was close by. A second later, she and Michael were inside the dome and Adali was hovering in front of them.

'Hello, beautiful,' said Molly.

Adali chirped.

'Wow,' said Michael. 'I don't think I'll ever get sick of this place.'

The facility looked the same as Molly remembered it. The high, dome-shaped ceiling let in the morning light, illuminating the plants throughout the space. But she turned her back on them to face the vine-covered wall. She stepped through and, a moment later, she was on the other side. Her father gasped then pulled her toward him.

'Muppet!' he said, kissing the top of her head.

'It's okay, Dad,' said Molly, wrapping her arms around his waist.

For a moment, she thought her father might start sobbing.

'We're going through now, Dad,' she said. 'Just you and me.'

'Okay,' he whispered.

A moment later, they were inside the dome, standing beside Michael and Adali. Molly's father gasped again.

'This is astonishing!' he said.

While he gazed around the space, Molly took the opportunity to slip through the wall again. Outside, Yosia and Gideon were pretending to fight. Their fists were raised, and their feet were shuffling back and forth. Yosia lifted his leg and swung sideways, performing a kick-boxing move but he slipped and fell into the wet mud. Eddie and Gideon laughed so loud; they almost blocked out the sound of the waterfalls.

'Aren't you guys a bit old for that kind of thing?' Molly asked.

'Ha-ha,' said Gideon, helping Yosia to his feet. 'Old man Yosia.'

Molly noticed Sergeant Nalong sitting quietly, fiddling with his phone.

'Are you receiving a reception here, Sergeant?' she asked.

'No, Molly,' he replied. 'I'm just setting my camera to panorama.'

Molly was not sure what *panorama* meant. She only hoped the sergeant, and anyone with a camera, would take detailed photos of everything inside the dome.

Yosia squeezed the water from his shirt then smiled at Molly.

'I'll take Eddie and Gideon through,' he said.

Molly watched Yosia wrap one arm around Eddie and the other around Gideon. A moment later, the three men were gone. She looked at Sergeant Nalong.

'Ready?' she asked.

'Yes,' he said, stepping behind her.

He placed his hands on her shoulders and she rested her heels on his toes.

'Okay, step forward,' she said.

The sergeant stepped forward. Soon, Molly felt her hands sinking into the soft gel. A moment later, she found herself inside the dome. Without Sergeant Nalong.

'Oh!' she said, looking around. 'What happened?'

Yosia frowned.

'That's strange,' he said. 'I'll go back for him.'

As Yosia slipped through the wall, Molly's father approached her.

'Are you okay, muppet?' he asked.

'Yes, thanks, Dad,' she replied.

But she could not take her eyes off the wall. She was trying to figure out what had happened to Sergeant Nalong. A second later, Yosia emerged through the wall. Alone.

'That's odd,' he said, looking around.

'What's going on?' Eddie demanded.

Adali landed on Yosia's shoulder and chirped in his ear. He listened for a moment, then nodded at the group huddled in front of him.

'The wall seems to have its own reasons for leaving Sergeant Nalong outside,' he said.

'What?' said Eddie. 'I'm not leaving him out there alone!'

Everyone stared at Eddie.

'I have an idea,' said Yosia.

He slipped through the wall again.

Molly's father pointed at Adali, now perched on Michael's shoulder.

'Did that bird just speak to Yosia?' he asked.

Molly and Michael exchanged glances. Molly saw a tiny smile lift the corners of the boy's mouth, but she felt too nervous to smile back. She knew her father would find it impossible to accept the notion of a talking bird. The fact that he was standing in an invisible, top-secret research facility would have been enough for him.

Yosia emerged through the wall again.

'Well, we tried again and failed again,' he said. 'For whatever reason, the wall does not want Sergeant Nalong to enter.'

'Why not?' Eddie demanded.

Yosia shrugged.

'It's a living organism,' he replied. 'It makes its own decisions. We don't need to know its reasons to honor them. Besides, the sergeant said he was happy to wait outside.'

Eddie's shoulders slumped.

'Ah well,' he said. 'There are six of us; enough to get the job done.'

'There's just one thing we need to be careful of,' said Michael.

Everyone looked at the boy.

'Whatever you do, don't step on the soil,' he said. 'Unless you want to set off the alarm.'

Everyone looked at Molly.

'Yes, it's true,' she said. 'That's how I set off the alarm last time.'

'Okay,' said Molly's father, looking at Eddie. 'What's the collection plan?'

Adali left Yosia's shoulder and flew to the far side of the dome.

'I'm following her,' said Yosia.

As Molly watched Yosia scuttle down the grey concrete path after Adali, she hoped they would find the evidence Adali had seen the previous evening. But in this place, she knew, anything would be possible.

19

COLLECTING THE EVIDENCE

Eddie removed his backpack then pulled out a bundle of plastic bags.

'One for each of you,' he said, handing them around.

Gideon was the first to unroll his. Then he played with the zip-lock seal; opening and closing it several times, while everyone watched.

'Just as well it's not bubble wrap,' said Molly.

Eddie laughed, then turned his attention to the group.

'Okay, folks, here's the plan,' he said. 'The four of you should spread out as far away from each other as possible and collect one leaf from every type of plant you see. If you can get a soil sample without setting off the alarm, that would be great. I'll move around the place, taking photographs, and if I find any water, I—'

'There's a pond near the center,' said Molly.

Michael laughed.

'Be careful though, Eddie,' he said. 'It's full of zombie frogs.'

'Zombie frogs?' Eddie echoed. 'I can't say I've ever heard of zombie frogs.'

'It's true,' said Molly. 'Their eyes are clouded over, like something dead. But they're not dead because they open their mouths and suction onto your skin. They're gross, but they don't bite. You just need to pull them off your skin and throw them back into the pond.'

'How do you know this?' asked Molly's father.

'We fell into the pond the first time we were here,' Molly replied. 'By the time we climbed out, we were covered in them.' she added with a shiver of disgust.

Molly's father clenched his jaw and shook his head.

'It's just one horror story after another with you kids,' he said.

Eddie cleared his throat.

'We should get this done in fifteen minutes,' he said. 'In fact, let's meet back here in ten.'

Everyone nodded then walked away in different directions.

Molly found herself following a path that veered toward the far-left side of the dome, realizing she had not been on this side of the dome during her last two visits. Beside her was a cluster of bamboo trees. Their trunks were grey, like any mature bamboo tree, but they were only a couple of meters tall. There were no leaves on the trunks, but at the top of each tree was a thick mop of bright turquoise leaves. They were the same color as the vine growing up the wall of the dome and some of the plants she remembered seeing inside the volcano. The contaminated lakes inside the volcano and mine were also the same color, which made her wonder if there was a contaminated lake right here, in the floor of the dome.

She wished Michael was beside her, so she could

discuss it with him. Then she remembered something Eddie had said the previous day - his analysis of the contaminated lakes had shown that 1% was a mysterious chemical he had not been able to identify. Where are they making this chemical, she wondered. Here, inside the dome? Or inside the mine? Inside the volcano, perhaps? Or in another top-secret location?

Molly desperately wanted to collect a leaf from the bamboo, but they were too high for her to reach. So she kneeled down and lifted a clump of topsoil near the edge of the path. She dropped it into her collection bag, remembering how awful it had been when she had set off the alarm the last time she had been here. It had happened because she had crawled too far into the patch of soil, toward the yellow ball that had been sitting there.

She saw a yellow ball now, too, nestled between the trunks of the bamboo. Then she saw another one and another. Placed at regular intervals, two meters apart, she still found them just as intriguing as the last time she had been in the dome. She wanted to stick the corner of her plastic bag inside one of the balls, to take a sample of whatever was inside it, because she felt certain it would help Eddie's analysis. But she could not risk it. The alarm would be too awful to listen to and it would put her entire team at risk, so she retreated.

She was just about to walk away she heard a strange sound. At first, she thought it was a bird, but then she remembered the only bird inside the dome was Adali. And if Adali wanted to make her presence known, she would have done so. The sound moved through the bamboo again. This time, Molly thought it sounded like a cat mewling.

'Puss, puss,' she whispered.

She heard the sound a third time. This time, she got the feeling it was not an animal, but a person. It sounded like the muffled cries of someone who could not speak.

'Who's there?' she whispered.

She heard the sound a fourth time. It was longer, of a lower pitch and more desperate.

'It's okay,' Molly whispered again. 'I'll help you.'

But she could not see how to get to the sound without stomping through the bamboo trees and triggering the alarm, so she lay on the concrete path and gazed between the trunks of the trees. On the far side of the cluster, she saw another grey concrete path. Upon it stood four steel legs glistening under the morning light. They were the legs of a chair, she knew, but she could not see anyone's feet beside them.

'Is someone there?' she asked.

She heard the sound again; just as desperate as before.

'Hold on!' she said. 'I'm coming for you!'

Molly jumped to her feet and ran down the path, hoping to find a way to access the source of the pained cry. When she spotted a narrow path veering off to the left, she leapt onto it at such speed, she almost slid into the soil. The path was so narrow; the leaves on both sides were whipping her cheeks as she ran past them. But the narrow path soon veered off to the left, and opened wide, and that's when she saw the strangest thing.

A steel chair, much higher than herself, stood in the center of the path about fifteen meters ahead. On it sat something shaped like a human body. It was difficult to tell at first, but as Molly got closer, she recognized the wild mane of frizzy grey hair as Mrs. Calthorpe's. But it was the back of the woman's head, and she was not moving. She stopped, terrified of what she might see if she got closer. Was Mrs. Calthorpe dead, she wondered. If so, would she look horrible and scary?

Suddenly, the woman wriggled and cried out again, so Molly ran toward her. Soon she was close enough to touch Mrs. Calthorpe's elbow. A moment later, she was standing in front of her. The woman's skin was almost porcelain white, and she seemed to have more wrinkles that usual. Her eyes were red and filled with tears. Her shirt was torn, and a black scarf had been tied across her mouth so tightly, it had disappeared between her lips. Her hands were tied to the arms of the chair and her feet were tied to its legs.

'Oh, Mrs. Calthorpe,' she gasped. 'Don't worry. I'm going to untie you, now.'

But it was not easy because the arms of the chair were as high as Molly's shoulders.

'I need Michael,' she said.

Mrs. Calthorpe nodded, so Molly took in a deep breath and turned her face upward.

'Michael!' she shouted. 'Help!'

She hoped that would be enough to grab the boy's attention, then she used every bit of strength in her fingers to untie the rope around Mrs. Calthorpe's left ankle.

'Molly?' she heard Michael holler.

'Over here!' Molly shouted. 'Hurry!'

Finally, she removed the rope from Mrs. Calthorpe's left ankle. The woman groaned with relief as she stretched her leg and made little circles with her foot.

'Does that feel better?' she asked, smiling at the woman.

But all she saw in Mrs. Calthorpe's eyes was fear, as

the woman glared at something on the path behind Molly. The footsteps pounding behind Molly were Michael's, she knew, but when she turned to greet him, all she saw was a huge body lunging toward her. She felt two hands grab her shoulders and lift her off the ground. She looked up at flabby jowls hanging from a chin. Jimbo's chin.

'I should have known you'd be behind this!' Molly shouted, kicking her legs.

But Jimbo was fast, especially for someone so large, and he managed to avoid Molly's kicks. Before Molly knew it, he had lowered her to the ground behind Mrs. Calthorpe's chair. He picked up the discarded rope and brought it to Molly's wrist. She knew he was going to tie her to the back of the chair.

'Get off me!' she shrieked, using every bit of power in her body to push him away.

But Jimbo was much faster and stronger.

'This must be my lucky day,' he said.

Molly could see his grey and crooked teeth and she could smell the stink of cigarettes and coffee on his breath.

'You won't get away with this!' she shrieked.

And she was right. Another large body appeared. It was not as large as Jimbo, but almost. It burst through the cluster of bamboo trees, then leapt on top of Jimbo, forcing him to the ground. By the time Molly realized it was Michael, the boy was sitting on Jimbo's chest, squeezing the air out of the man's lungs. Michael raised his right elbow and clenched his fist, then planted a savage punch on the side of Jimbo's mouth.

'I've been wanting to do that for a long time,' he said, raising his elbow again.

Molly wondered why the alarm had not gone off, but she had more important things to worry about, like untying Mrs. Calthorpe. The woman's eyes were pouring with tears, and she was still struggling to break free. Molly wanted to pull the awful scarf from Mrs. Calthorpe's mouth, but she could not reach, so she did the next best thing. Standing on her tiptoes, she started to untie the rope from the woman's left wrist.

'Don't worry, Mrs. Calthorpe,' she said. 'I'll have you free in a second.'

Molly felt all her fingernails breaking as she pulled at the knot, but she kept going.

'Molly?' she heard her father call out. 'Where are you?'

'Over here, Dad!' Molly shouted. 'Hurry!'

She glanced at Michael just in time to see him landing on his back on the concrete path. The boy groaned, which made Mrs. Calthorpe wriggle even more. As Jimbo stood over Michael, Molly wanted to run to her friend's rescue, but she knew she would be crushed in the kerfuffle, so she kept working on the knot. A moment later, the rope fell to the ground.

Mrs. Calthorpe brought her hand to her face and pulled the scarf below her chin.

'Don't you hurt my boy!' she screamed.

She could not see the fight, but Molly could, and she was horrified. She saw Jimbo lunge toward Michael, and that made her work even faster to untie the knot around Mrs. Calthorpe's right ankle.

'Michael's fine,' she lied.

But Mrs. Calthorpe did not believe her. She started wriggling so much, she almost tilted the chair sideways.

'You're making it worse!' said Molly, tugging at the knot.

She heard her father behind her.

'Jimbo!' he shouted. 'Leave the boy alone!'

Mrs. Calthorpe tried to twist her body around to see what was happening between Jimbo and Michael, but she could not reach. She started gasping. It was not fear or exhaustion that made her gasp, Molly knew, but rage.

'If you hurt my boy, Jimbo, I swear I will ki—' she shrieked.

Molly's father ran past them so fast, he seemed to fly. Molly watched him, astonished, as he grabbed the back of Jimbo's legs and brought him to the ground.

'Good one, Dad!' she squealed.

She pulled the rope away from Mrs. Calthorpe's right ankle just as the woman pulled another rope away from her right wrist and leaped out of the chair. She dashed toward the scramble of male limbs on the ground, but Molly stopped her.

'No!' she said, grabbing Mrs. Calthorpe's arm. 'You'll get hurt!'

Molly watched her father restrain Jimbo's legs while Michael restrained the man's wrists.

'Give me that rope, Molly!' her father shouted.

Molly collected the fallen pieces of rope and used one to tie Jimbo's ankles together. At that moment, Yosia and Gideon skidded around the corner.

'Hurry!' Molly shouted at them.

She could see that Michael's hands, wet with sweat, were losing their grip on Jimbo's wrists. Suddenly, his grip was broken, and Jimbo's arms were free. He whacked the side of Michael's face with the back of his muscular forearm.

'No!' Mrs. Calthorpe screamed.

As Michael fell, Yosia raced past him, dropped to his knees, and forced his entire body weight upon Jimbo's wrists. Gideon ran to Molly's father and helped him hold Jimbo's legs while Molly continued to bind them.

'Dad, you'll have to tie the knots tighter,' she said.

She stood back then, close to Mrs. Calthorpe, watching Michael crawl back toward Jimbo's thrashing body. The boy kneeled beside Yosia and used a piece of rope to bind Jimbo's wrists, while Yosia held them steady. Finally, Jimbo was restrained.

Molly's father wiped the sweat off his brow, then smiled at her and Mrs. Calthorpe.

'Are you two okay?' he asked.

'We are,' Molly replied.

Jimbo sat up, glared at Molly, and spat out a long string of foul words.

'I don't have to listen to that!' she said.

Molly took the crumpled and saliva-soaked scarf from Mrs. Calthorpe's hand, pressed it into Jimbo's mouth and tied it behind his head as tightly as she could.

'That's better,' she said, standing up.

Jimbo was now completely helpless, and everyone breathed a sigh of relief. Michael ran toward his mother while Molly crawled across the soil toward the yellow ball.

'What are you doing, muppet?' her father asked.

'Taking advantage of the fact that the alarm is switched off!' she replied.

She wrapped her hands around the ball and pulled hard. Suddenly she heard a *snap!* and the thing broke free. From what, she did not know.

'Dad! Catch!' she shouted, throwing the mysterious object toward him.

He caught it with his plastic bag.

'Good one, Dad!' she said.

Then she dug into the soil as fast and deep as she could.

'Come on, Molly,' her father groaned. 'That's enough.'

But like a dog seeking a buried bone, Molly kept digging. And then she saw it - a network of black plastic pipes. Arranged in a logical matrix structure, they met at a central point, directly under the yellow ball. Whatever those pipes had been delivering to the ball was in her father's collection bag, she knew, and that was good enough.

'Come on!' she heard him shout.

There was an edge to his tone which, she knew, meant he was losing patience with her, so she crawled back. Soon she felt his hands on her waist then he pulled her to her feet and wrapped his arms around her.

'I'm so glad you're okay, muppet,' he said.

Molly saw Michael and his mother hugging. Mrs. Calthorpe was sobbing.

'I'm so sorry, Michael,' she blubbered. 'I'm so sorry.'

'Shh, Mum,' he said. 'It's okay.'

Yosia stood up and wiped the sweat from his face. Adali sat on his shoulder, her head cocked to the side. Gideon stood over Jimbo, looking down at him.

'I never liked you,' he said.

'I never liked him, either,' said Yosia.

'No one likes him,' Molly scoffed.

'Okay, guys, that's enough,' said Molly's father. 'Let's

not make things worse. Jimbo will pay for his actions a thousand times over. I will see to it, personally.'

Then he stepped over to Jimbo and stared into the man's tiny eyes.

'You were a trusted colleague, Jimbo,' he said. 'And you've betrayed that trust.'

Jimbo sighed then closed his eyes.

'I'm taking Mum back to the vehicle,' said Michael. 'She needs food and water.'

Everyone nodded their agreement as Michael wrapped his arm around his mother's waist and led her away from the ghastly steel chair that had held her captive. For how long, Molly did not know because there had been no time to ask. She watched them go, feeling satisfied that Sergeant Nalong would be outside waiting for them.

But they would have to get through the wall, first.

'Hang on!' she shouted. 'I'll help you out!'

'Just be careful, muppet,' her father said, slowly letting her go.

'I will!' Molly replied.

When she caught up with Michael and his mother, Molly suddenly thought about Eddie. Why had he not arrived to help them, she wondered. All the noise they made must have caught his attention, she figured.

'Michael, did you see Eddie before you came to our rescue?' she asked.

'No,' he replied.

As they approached the agreed meeting place, Molly glanced around, hoping to see Eddie. But he was not there. She decided to help Mrs. Calthorpe outside first, then return to search for Eddie.

'I'll have you out of here in a second, Mrs. Calthorpe,' she said.

The woman scowled at her.

'Don't tell me you kids have stolen a laser gun!' she hissed.

'No! Of course not!' Molly replied.

'Trust us, Mum, we know what we're doing,' said Michael.

Less than a meter from the wall, Molly wrapped one arm around Michael and another around Mrs. Calthorpe.

'But—' the woman muttered as they entered the soft gel.

A moment later, they were standing outside in the wet mud, surrounded by the noise of the waterfalls crashing down the wall of the sinkhole.

20

WE GOT THE BAD GUYS

'What the—' Mrs. Calthorpe started.

But her attention was immediately taken by a commotion at the base of the steps. Sergeant Nalong was engaged in combat with three men dressed in white jumpsuits.

'Oh, no. Not these guys,' she groaned.

'Who are they, Mum?' Michael asked.

'Scientists from Symbiotica,' she replied.

Michael's shoulders slumped.

'We have to do something,' he said.

'No, we don't,' said Mrs. Calthorpe. 'We've been through enough.'

Sergeant Nalong fell to the ground, face first. He landed so heavily; Molly saw ripples in the mud around his head.

'Leave him alone!' she shrieked.

But the sergeant was quick to get back on his feet, and even quicker to plant a kick on the leg of the nearest Symbiotica scientist. The man fell, screaming and clutching his knee. Molly tugged on the sleeve of Michael's t-shirt.

'Call Adali!' she shouted.

'What?' Mrs. Calthorpe scoffed. 'Yosia's pet bird?'

Michael pulled on the leather strap around his neck, releasing the little wooden carving of the bird. Then he wrapped his hand around it and shouted: 'Adali! Please help!'

'Michael, what are you doing?' asked Mrs. Calthorpe.

Before Michael could answer, Molly took the woman's arm and gently led her away.

'Come on, Mrs. Calthorpe,' she said. 'There's nothing we can do. And you need water.'

With some resistance, Mrs. Calthorpe allowed Molly to bring her to the main waterfall.

'Michael!' the woman called out.

But her voice was fading, and her body was becoming heavier.

'I know you're exhausted, but we're nearly there,' said Molly.

A moment later, Molly and Mrs. Calthorpe were wading through the knee-deep pool of white water. The sprays and splashes leaped through air, reminding Molly of the joy she had felt when she and Michael had first discovered this oasis.

'Can you feel that?' she asked.

Mrs. Calthorpe grunted, then called for Michael again.

'I'm here, Mum,' he said, leaping through the pool.

He wrapped his arm around his mother's back and turned her away from the fighting men. But Molly looked back at the commotion, and what she saw made her smile. Adali was hovering above the Symbiotica scientists, casting her bright white light around them. Suddenly, they were encased, mid-movement, in the light. A moment later, the light transformed into a semi-transparent gel, holding them firmly in place. The next moment, they were no longer visible.

'Oh, this is so good,' Mrs. Calthorpe groaned as the waterfall completely drenched her.

Michael glanced at the base of steps where the scientists had been. Then he looked at Molly, smiled and winked.

'Can I leave you here for a minute?' Molly asked.

'What for?'

'I need to find Eddie,' Molly replied. 'And Sergeant Nalong still needs help.'

'Okay,' said Michael.

Molly ran to Sergeant Nalong. He was sitting in the wet mud, his mouth was open, staring at nothing. She wrapped her hands around one of his muscular arms and helped him to his feet.

'Is this the first time you've seen this?' she asked.

'Seen what?' the sergeant replied, unable to break his gaze on the place where the three scientists had been standing a moment earlier. 'They were just there,' he whispered, pointing. 'Then the bird turned up and now they're gone.'

'They're still there,' Molly explained. 'You just can't see them because Adali has created an invisible shield around them.'

'What?' the sergeant snapped.

'Just as the research facility is right here, and surrounded by an invisible shield,' Molly continued.

'Those three scientists are encased inside an invisible shield.'

'Really?' said Sergeant Nalong.

'Yes,' said Molly. 'We can discuss it later, but first we need to find Eddie.'

'Where is he?' the sergeant sputtered.

'Somewhere inside the dome,' Molly replied. 'Shall we try to enter together?'

Sergeant Nalong's face fell.

'But the wall wouldn't let me in,' he said. 'Remember?'

'I have a feeling it will change its mind,' said Molly. 'Come on, put your arm around me.'

Together, they stepped through the wall. Once inside, Sergeant Nalong gasped.

'This is even more incredible than anything I had—' he started.

Yosia and Gideon stepped onto the central path, dragging Jimbo between them. The awful man was not even trying to hop. He was allowing his entire body weight flop, making it difficult for Yosia and Gideon to move him.

'What's going on here?' asked Sergeant Nalong.

'That's Jimbo,' Molly replied. 'He's a nasty piece of work. He abducted Mrs. Calthorpe, tied her up and left her over there,' she added, pointing to the far side of the dome.

The sergeant stepped toward the three men.

'Do you guys need help with this menace?' he asked.

They shook their heads.

'We'll have him out of here in a moment,' said Yosia.

'Just dump him next to the three Symbiotica dudes outside,' said Molly.

'What?' said Yosia.

'Sergeant Nalong was attacked by them, but Adali has contained them now,' Molly explained.

Yosia smiled.

'About that—' the sergeant started.

'I promise I'll explain everything,' said Molly. 'For now, though, we need to find Eddie. I'd also like to know where my dad is. Have you seen him, Yosia?'

'They're both in the office,' Yosia replied.

'Office?' Molly echoed. 'What office?'

'Over there,' Yosia replied, nodding at a neatly trimmed hedge of hibiscus trees.

Molly stared at it, wondering why she had never noticed it before.

'Um. That's not an office,' she said.

'On the other side of the hedge,' Yosia replied.

He wrapped one arm around Jimbo, clutching the man's shoulder so tightly, Molly felt certain it would hurt. Then he wrapped his other arm around Gideon.

'Come on, Giddy man,' he said. 'Let's get this nasty lump outside.'

Molly watched the three men disappear through the wall, then she turned her attention to Sergeant Nalong. The man looked completely bewildered.

'Ready?' she asked.

Sergeant Nalong seemed to be in a daze, staring around the incredible dome. She tugged his arm then ran toward the hedge. It must have been almost three meters high, she figured, and very thick.

'Dad!' she called out.

'Back here, muppet!' she heard him reply.

Molly ran around the hedge, suddenly astonished by what she saw. A long white desk rested against the wall of the dome. Upon it were several computer screens, each one active with columns of moving data. Eddie and her father were staring at it.

'Hey,' her father said, reaching his hand toward her.

She snuggled into him and stared at the screens.

'What's all this, Dad?' she asked.

'We think it's the results of a continuous monitoring system,' her father replied. 'There must be sensors throughout this place, monitoring the nutrition and growth of each plant.'

'Interesting,' said Molly. 'I guess we'll learn more about that when Eddie analyzes the contents of the yellow ball.'

'What yellow ball?' Eddie asked.

'I pulled one from the soil,' Molly replied. 'They're everywhere, about two meters apart, and they're all connected to an underground reticulation system.'

'I didn't even notice,' said Eddie. 'I'm grateful for your attention to detail, Molly.'

At the far end of the bench, Molly saw a large tub built into its surface.

'What do you suppose they've got in here?' she asked, peering into a barrel of bright turquoise water. 'Oh, my goodness. This is where they make the mysterious chemical you haven't been able to identify yet, Eddie.'

'Indeed, it is,' said Eddie.

'What's this?' Sergeant Nalong asked, pointing to a lump of black plastic.

Molly figured it would have been about the same size as her school lunchbox.

'I reckon it's the main computer,' she said.

'Yes, it is,' said Eddie. 'I've already downloaded the data, but let me show you now, Molly.'

Molly watched him open several documents at once.

'But how did you access this computer?' she asked. 'I mean, it must have passwords and stuff.'

Eddie looked down for a moment then scratched his head.

'I used to be a hacker,' he said.

'Oh, wow!' said Molly. 'That's so cool!'

Eddie shook his head.

'Not cool, Molly,' he said. 'I spent a couple of years in prison for my crimes.'

Sergeant Nalong patted Eddie's back so gently, it reminded Molly of the way her mother always patted her back when she needed comfort. She wished her mother was here with her now, joining the adventure.

'Anyway,' said Eddie. 'There's evidence here of everything you've known all along, Molly.'

'What do you mean?' she asked.

'Plans for agromining as a substitute for underground mining,' Eddie replied, scrolling through one of the documents. 'But instead of allowing plants to absorb the metals naturally, Symbiotica has been inventing plants that will do it faster. And they're feeding those plants with this mysterious chemical we haven't been able to identify.'

'Yep,' said Molly. 'It's just as we suspected.'

'No, it's as *you* suspected,' Eddie argued.

Molly felt her father gently squeeze her shoulders.

'There are also records of Symbiotica's scientists creating animals that could live off the plants that are fed this chemical,' Eddie continued. 'It seems the Jeffries did something to interrupt that project, and that's why they were forced to leave.'

'Let's hope the Jeffries made it back home safe and sound,' said Molly's father.

Eddie looked up at him and shook his head.

'I haven't been able to find any information about them,' he said.

Then he opened another document.

'Listen to this,' he said. 'The animal experimentation got *out of hand*, whatever that means, so the animals were *disposed of*,' he said.

'Disposed of?' Molly shouted.

'Don't panic,' said Eddie. 'They go on to say the animals were relocated and left to develop naturally. I think we all know that means they were put inside the volcano. Ah, I deeply regret not having the courage to photograph those beasts inside the volcano.'

'Give yourself a break, Eddie man,' said Sergeant Nalong, patting Eddie's back again. 'It's not safe down there. I'm horrified you ventured anywhere near the place.'

'Molly and Michael had the courage to explore it,' Eddie argued.

'Yes, but they were out of order, and they knew no better,' said Molly's father.

Molly scowled at him.

'I think it's time we left now,' said Sergeant Nalong.

Eddie switched off the computer then stood up.

'I've downloaded all the data from this computer onto this,' he said, tapping his watch.

'Awesome,' said Molly.

'Come on, now,' said Sergeant Nalong, almost dragging Eddie away from the computer.

'Did you get a sample of the turquoise liquid from this barrel?' Molly asked.

'Yup! It's in my backpack,' Eddie replied, sliding his arms through the straps.

'What about the slimy green pond?' Molly asked.

'That, too,' Eddie replied, walking around the hedge. 'Oh, and while I was at it, I found those zombie frogs you mentioned.'

'Aren't they gross?' Molly squealed.

'They sure are,' said Eddie, following the sergeant toward the exit point. 'But I was lucky to find a dead one, so I put it in my collection bag which is also in my backpack.'

Molly stopped for a moment, realizing her face was too close to Eddie's backpack.

'I'm glad I won't be putting my hands in there!' she said.

'Don't you like zombie frog soup?' Eddie asked.

'Gross!' Molly squealed.

When they reached the wall, Molly said: 'I have an idea.' She decided to try and transport them through the wall using Yosia's technique. She wrapped one arm around her father and the other around Eddie then said: 'Sergeant, how about you stand behind me and put your hand on my shoulder? We should all go through together.'

She soon felt the sergeant's hand on her shoulder.

'All aboard,' she giggled as she stepped forward.

A moment later, she was outside the dome with her father and Eddie.

'Oh, no,' she laughed. 'Poor Sergeant Nalong has been left behind again!'

Molly was about to enter the dome again when she

saw a long dark object falling down the waterfall. Its head was pointing at the pool of white below and its body was wriggling from side to side.

'Ted!' she squealed. 'Look, everyone! It's Ted!'

The great lizard made a huge splash but was quick to find his feet and wade out of the pool.

'Ted!' Molly squealed again, dropping to her knees.

The lizard ambled toward her, staring straight at her through his fluorescent blue eyes. His pace was calm and relaxed, just as Molly remembered, but she sensed something different. It was the same thing she had sensed the night she had found him in her laundry closet. Rage.

'Get back, Molly,' her father said, stepping in front of her.

But Molly stepped around her father because she wanted to see her old friend. She had missed him, and she was curious about his transformation. She wanted to touch him, but Gideon stepped between them.

'No, Molly,' he said. 'It's not safe.'

Gideon stared at Ted while pointing to a crack in the rock wall.

'Go on,' he said.

Ted stood up on his back legs, spread his claws and hissed, just had as he had done when he had defended Molly from the scary dinosaur inside the volcano. Molly felt her father's hand wrap around her wrist as he pulled her behind him, again.

'Go, Ted,' said Gideon.

Slowly, Ted returned to his four feet and ambled toward to the rock wall.

'Surely he's come to help us,' Molly argued.

'Perhaps,' said Gideon. 'But he's not stable enough to

do much good. He could snap at any second. Trust me Molly, I've been watching him for a while.'

Molly watched Ted leave, her throat tightening and her eyes filling with tears.

'Ted,' she whispered.

The great lizard turned around, gazed at her again then crawled into the crack between the rocks. As the tip of his tail disappeared inside the tiny cave, Molly felt her tears fall down her face. She felt terrible to see her old friend so alone and confused by the awful chemical bath he had endured inside the volcano.

Trying not to cry, Molly turned her attention to Sergeant Nalong.

'Do you have phone reception yet, Sergeant?' she asked.

'No,' the sergeant replied. 'But I will when we get out of this hole. I'll call for police back up. And a Medical Officer.'

'Don't forget to tell them about the three scientists bundled up here,' said Molly, pointing at the side of the steps.

The sergeant frowned, so Molly stepped over to the place where she had last seen the three men bundled together in a blob of gel. She kicked her foot into that place, and the tip of her foot disappeared.

'See?' she said.

The sergeant shook his head and laughed.

'Adali will reveal them to the police,' said Yosia.

Molly looked around and noticed everyone was looking at her.

'I guess you're all waiting for me to get you to the top,' she said.

Several people nodded.

'Molly, could you please help my mum out first?' Michael asked. 'She hasn't eaten for twenty-four hours.'

Molly raced up the steps and helped Mrs. Calthorpe to her feet. Then she looked over her shoulder, happy to see everyone following. Yosia and Gideon were behind her, lugging Jimbo up the steps. Her father was behind them. And behind him, were Eddie and Sergeant Nalong, holding hands. All Molly had to do next was get them out of the sinkhole.

21

WHAT NEXT?

Slowly, the motley crew of nine people shuffled across the bright green valley toward the big white vehicle. Then, one by one, they slumped on the grass, groaning with exhaustion. Except for Sergeant Nalong, who wandered toward the back of the vehicle. He returned a moment later, carrying a large white box. Then he placed it on the grass and lifted the lid.

'This is full of fresh food and cool drinks,' he said. 'I suggest we consume everything, so we can use the ice to store the samples you've all collected.'

'Sounds good to me,' said Michael, reaching into the box.

He pulled out a wrapped plate containing a piece of chicken and some salad, removed the wrapper and gave it to his mother.

'Please eat, Mum,' he said.

While everyone else reached into the box for food and drinks, Molly gathered the collection bags. By the time she reached the ice box, all food and drinks had been removed, so she dumped the bags on top of the ice and shut the lid.

'Too easy!' she sang, sitting beside her father.

'Drink up, muppet,' he said, handing her a small carton of orange juice.

As Molly brought the straw to her mouth, she glanced at her father and winked at him. For the next few moments, she noticed that all conversation had been replaced by the sounds of people eating and drinking. The sun was about halfway up the sky, and the heat was increasing so it felt like the perfect moment for an unplanned picnic.

'What about Jimbo?' she asked.

Yosia pointed his water bottle at Jimbo and squeezed it, causing a jet of water to hit the nasty man in the mouth. It was a small action, but one that Molly found hilarious, so she laughed out loud. A moment later, Eddie sighed, and everyone looked at him.

'What's up?' Michael asked.

'I'm just thinking about all the work I have to do,' Eddie replied. 'I need to test all these samples, write up my findings then write a briefing paper for my Member of Parliament and send it to her with a request to meet with her. Oh, then I will have to prepare my presentation to her and her team and—'

'Practice presentation on us!' said Molly. 'We can add anything you might have missed.'

Eddie's face lit up.

'That would be great!' he said. 'How's tomorrow morning at your place, Mr. Marsh?'

'Eddie, man, please slow down,' said Sergeant Nalong. 'Let's deal with one thing at a time. The police will be here in an hour or so. They will interview each of us separately and record our statements. After that, everyone will need some rest, especially Mrs. Calthorpe.'

Eddie nodded.

'Fair enough,' he said. 'Perhaps I was getting ahead of myself.'

'It's understandable,' said Molly's father. 'There's a lot to be done. If there's anything I can do, please don't hes—'

'Oh, will you look at that fool!' said Mrs. Calthorpe, pointing across the valley.

Everyone looked. There was Jimbo, almost fifty meters away, lying on the ground.

'Is he really trying to escape?' Michael laughed.

Jimbo got to his knees then pressed his hands into the ground and forced himself to a standing position. Then like a person in a potato sack race, he slowly started hopping away.

'How ridiculous,' said Eddie.

Molly saw something moving at the base of the mountain. It had long black legs and a mound of black and white feathers.

'It's a cassowary!' Michael laughed.

Jimbo turned around and started to hop back toward the safety of the group. But he was not quick enough. In seconds, the cassowary had caught up to him and knocked him to the ground. He started thrashing around, but that did nothing to concern the bird. Instead, the cassowary took one step onto Jimbo's lumpy back. Then another. Then it bounced up and down, as though the man were a trampoline.

'What's it doing?' Molly laughed.

The bouncing continued for several seconds while everyone roared with laughter. And with every bounce, the cassowary leapt higher. Soon, it leapt so high, Jimbo had just enough time to roll away. But the great bird was quick to leap upon him again and continue its fun.

'Perhaps Jimbo will be more docile after a good stomping,' Michael sobbed with laughter.

'Actually, I'm a bit worried,' said her father. 'Those birds can kill.'

'True,' said Yosia.

The cassowary slowed its rate of bouncing, then stopped. For a moment, it just stood there, its head cocked to the side. It lifted one foot and pointed a sharp claw at the back of Jimbo's neck. Then it lowered its claw while everyone gasped. Molly felt her gut clench as she realized she was about to witness someone being killed.

'Don't look, muppet!' her father said.

But Molly could not stop looking. She saw a tiny brown speck circling the cassowary's head. She knew it was Adali, even though she had not seen her friend fly over there. The cassowary shook its head, ruffled its feathers then ran back toward the jungle-covered mountain.

'I definitely have some questions about Yosia's bird,' said Molly's father.

For the next few seconds, Jimbo just lay there.

'Do you think he's dead?' Molly asked.

'I don't know,' her father replied. 'Yosia, what shall we do?'

Yosia whistled at Adali. Still hovering over Jimbo, the bird circled down toward his head. A moment later, the big man began rolling back toward the group.

'I also have questions about Yosia's bird,' said Sergeant Nalong.

'Oh, we all have questions about a lot of things,' said Molly. 'Actually, I have millions. In fact, I'm going to make a long list of them tonight before I go to sleep.'

'You'll make a great forensic scientist one day,' said Eddie.

Molly did not know what *forensic* meant, but she was happy to hear the word *scientist*.

'We all have something we can do to help you, Eddie,' said Mrs. Calthorpe. 'Especially me,' she added with a sigh.

Molly thought the woman's expression looked sad and full of regret, and she felt sorry for her. But she hoped Mrs. Calthorpe would finally be ready to share Symbiotica's dirty secrets. For now, though, she just had one question.

'Mrs. Calthorpe, do you know why Jimbo took you to the dome and tied you up?' she asked.

The woman's bottom lip quivered, as though she was about to cry.

'I'm sorry,' said Molly. 'I shouldn't ask so many questions.'

'It's okay,' said Mrs. Calthorpe. 'I'll provide a detailed statement to the police, but for now, I can tell you that Jimbo was acting on orders from someone very senior at Symbiotica. They wanted Jimbo to dispose of me because I had been asking too many questions.'

Michael shook his head and gripped his mother's hand. Then he glared at Jimbo who was still hopping toward the group. Molly saw a darkness sweep across Michael's face, and she knew it meant trouble. Michael would want revenge on Jimbo for hurting his mother, she knew.

Then Molly's father cleared his throat so suddenly, everyone looked at him.

'I have something to say,' he announced. 'I would like to acknowledge my brave and brilliant daughter, without whom, I would be blissfully ignorant of so many things.'

Molly heard a crackle of emotion in his voice, and she leaned against his arm.

'I'm going to add to that,' said Michael. 'Since Molly came along, less than two weeks ago, my life has been turned upside down and inside out. I've never had a friend who gets me into so much trouble. She's a big pain in the butt, but I—'

Mrs. Calthorpe whacked Michael's arm to stop him from saying anything else. Then she turned to face Molly and said: 'Molly, you are the fire that keeps us all moving. Without your constant curiosity and relentless determination to uncover the truth of things, we'd be half asleep.'

Molly felt her face flush.

'I have something to add,' said Yosia.

'Oh, no,' said Molly, dropping her head into her hands.

'During the last few decades, I've hosted many foreigners,' he said. 'In all that time, I have never met such a ferocious little tyrant, nor anyone with such sensitivity to the natural world.'

Molly's father wrapped his arm around her shoulder.

'It's the same in Australia,' he said. 'Her mother and I have been commenting on it for years.'

Molly felt her face flushing.

'Please stop,' she groaned. 'You're embarrassing me.'

'Oh, good,' said Michael. 'The first time I met Molly—'

'Seriously, Michael, stop,' said Mrs. Calthorpe, laughing.

She wrapped her arms around her son and pulled him close to her.

'There is no one I would like to acknowledge more than you, my darling son,' she said.

Molly saw the boy's eyes glisten with tears.

'You have been my rock,' Mrs. Calthorpe continued. 'Through all the mad ups and downs, all the hard work and all the mistakes I've made, the only constant in my life has been you, Michael. I love you, darling, and I promise to be a much better mum from now on.'

Michael dropped his box of food and wrapped his arms around his mother.

'I love you, too, Mum,' he blubbered.

Molly felt her throat tighten with emotion as she watched. This was the moment she had always hoped would come for Michael. For so long, he had been broken by his mother's absence. He had been craving her affection, and now he was receiving it in bucket loads. But her father interrupted the moment.

He got to his knees, opened his arms, and shouted: 'Group hug!'

Everyone dropped their food packets and huddled in. Molly felt her father's arm around her shoulders and Yosia's arm around her waist. Amidst the mess of eight bodies, eight heads, sixteen arms, and sixteen knees, Molly stared at the patch of bright green grass and knew she would remember this moment forever.

❄

I hope you enjoyed this third book in the collection of *Molly's Magical Adventures* books. The next one, *Magic of the Guardians* will be available by Easter 2022. To be notified of release dates, please join the author's mailing list via her website: vkmay.com

www.ingramcontent.com/pod-product-compliance
Lightning Source LLC
Chambersburg PA
CBHW021438080526
44588CB00009B/575